ALL THOSE IN FAVOR
SAY SOMETHING

ALL THOSE IN FAVOR SAY SOMETHING!

an affectionate exposé of women's clubs

and an appendix of
Instant Parliamentary Law

by RUNA ERWIN WARE

with cartoons by Charles Wickersham III

Geron-X, Inc.   Los Altos, Calif.

Published by Geron-X, Inc., Box 1108, Los Altos, Calif. 94022
Library of Congress catalog card No. 68-54862
Printed in the United States of America
    by The Colonial Press Inc., Clinton, Mass.

Dedicated to

my husband and sons,
who have always wondered
what really goes on at women's meetings

Contents

Foreword

The first woman's club in America could have begun like this.
During the cold winter of 1620 when the Pilgrims were having
trouble keeping warm at Plymouth Rock, the ladies decided to
do something about it. When ladies want fast action they always do the same thing—they organize a club. So, the Sisters
of the Mayflower came into being, their main purpose being to
prod the men into installing a little mud insulation in their
cold cabins.

At the first meeting, they elected a chairman who graciously
accepted the position with these words:

"I'll be glad to be your chairman, ladies. In many ways I feel
responsible for our plight here in this freezing weather. My
husband was navigator for the *Mayflower,* and if I had been
more insistent and made him listen to me, we wouldn't be
freezing up here at Plymouth Rock—we'd all be spending the
winter in Florida."

Whether or not that was the launching of the first women's
club, the ladies have been embarking steadily ever since. Actually a women's club was organized in Boston in 1702, the first
ever officially recorded in this country. Today an estimated

forty million women belong to clubs listed at state and national levels in our country.

American men have been attempting to disparage women's organizations ever since the Pilgrim fathers disapproved of Anne Hutchinson, who organized a women's theological discussion club in Boston in 1634. Poor Anne was banished from Boston for "Heresy and Sedition."

Today, however, women like Anne are appointed judges, or elected to Congress, or chosen president of the local woman's club or the United Fund drive. Women are in almost every known type of business, and they not only spend more money than men, but they own more property and securities.

In fact it has been said that we are living in a "Woman's World," to such an extent that when a man is born everyone asks, "How's the mother?" When he marries, they comment, "Wasn't the bride lovely!", and when he dies they all inquire, "How much did he leave his widow?"

Business women and housewives are members of organizations that promote better schools, health programs, social reforms, cultural improvements, beautification programs, homemaking, historical preservations, better labor laws, farm programs, and endless philanthropic projects. They join and support patriotic and fraternal auxiliaries, garden clubs, youth groups, civic, political, and religious organizations.

Ask any minister and he will tell you that the backbone of his church is the women's organization. The wife or the mother in a family generally is the one who guides her husband and children in the right direction of their religious faith through church activity. If Mother is involved, so is everyone else.

When a friend of mine was president of her church women's group, she received this answer from her small son when she asked him the question, "What is the Trinity?" "I know that one real good, Mama. It's what you talk about all the time . . . the Deacons and the Elders and the Women of the Church."

Informed, modern women would not want a return to the Nineteenth Century hush-hush attitude regarding any attraction between men and women, for in those days all Cupid did was to shoot Valentine darts at shy maidens and bashful suitors. The word "sex" was only used on printed forms along with name, address, and age.

Those who fought for the emancipation of women hoped that the removal of restrictions and hypocrisy would lead to a dignified and intelligent attitude toward sex. Instead, the explosive reaction of youth to a complete reversal of the old concepts has been even more dangerously foolish. With the assistance of the news media and lax conventions, the pendulum of decency has swung so far now that there seems a high chance that future generations will revert to a Sodom and Gomorrah existence, unless the women become sufficiently concerned.

The voices of forty million church and club women could wield much influence, in spite of the droll ways they sometimes have of reaching their goals.

If it sounds as if I am impressed by all of these things that American women have done and can do—I am. Otherwise, I would not have written a book about them. But this book is different: it tells not about how efficient they are, but lets you in on some of the daft things that happen while they are achieving some of these wonderful accomplishments. Let's see what *some* women do and say at *some* club meetings. Shall we?

The Evolution of a Club Spy

A women's club is a gathering of ladies who get together to learn how to do something they already know how to do, but do not have time to do because they have to attend so many women's club meetings.

Surely it was a man who dreamed up this definition. Most men, and even many female non club-joiners, never fail to snicker at the very mention of a women's club. This goes on in spite of the fact that never in history have women reached such a high level of recognition, or played so many important roles in world affairs. Much of this is accomplished through the medium of worthwhile women's organizations.

One of these critical and unsympathetic husbands vowed that when his wife died he was planning to mark her tombstone with this epitaph:

> Here lies my dear wife, Mary Beth,
> Slowly, but surely, clubbed to death.

It is true that some women, carried away with "good works," can overemphasize their club or church activities to the detriment and neglect of their families. Naturally this brings about malevolent reactions from disgruntled husbands. Complaining about the numerous church suppers his wife supervised, while he ate left-overs, one man paraphrased the old hymn like this, "When the rolls are passed up yonder, she'll be there."

Many of those "join everything" females who spread their time and talents too thin usually accomplish little besides having their names on the roll of every organization in town. On the other hand, the millions of dedicated club women who budget their time, mobilize their administrative brain power and leadership are extremely important to our country today.

If women are so well organized and accomplish such vast and important projects, and are (supposedly) better informed on rules of parliamentary procedure than men, why is it that people still smile, or even smirk, when women's clubs are mentioned? I believe I know the answer.

It is because women conduct their meetings, shall we say, *differently,* from men. Because they are women first, and club members second, they twist the rules about to suit themselves, and fiddle-de-dee to Mr. Robert and his nice little whatcha-callit book.

Many women look upon the fine points of parliamentary rules much as they regard recipes. Every good cook (female, that is) adds a pinch or two of this, and omits a few drops or teaspoons of that, to suit her fancy.

Once I gave detailed instructions on making a favorite crab meat casserole to a friend who had praised this tasty dish repeatedly. Afterwards at a luncheon at her home, she greeted me enthusiastically, "Darling! Guess what! I'm having your gorgeous casserole today." As we entered the dining room she confided in a whisper that she had made a few changes. Not being able to secure fresh crab meat she had substituted canned tuna fish; mushroom soup had been used in place of the delicate white sauce ("easier"); sherry wine and blanched almonds had been omitted ("forgot to put them on the grocery list"); boiled noodles had taken the place of steamed rice ("sounded better").

Seconds later, as our hostess plunged the serving spoon into the steaming pièce de résistance, she casually announced to the guests "Girls, if this casserole isn't any good, don't blame me. This is Runa Ware's recipe, not mine."

That little deviation from following rules might well apply to a club president whom I heard make this announcement: "I see everyone nodding their heads, so we won't bother to count the votes. I'm sure it is unanimous, and we are running late. People are already lining up in the dining room for the buffet. Meeting's adjourned, ladies."

Inconsistent? Out of order? Unbelievable? Incongruous? Call it what you may. The kindest and truest way to express it is that women are different . . . *very* different. "Enigma, thy name is woman" is never truer than when a lady chairman grasps a gavel in her hand and begins to pound.

Now . . . shall we go back a few years, and I will tell you the story of how and why I became so enthralled with this wonderful world of women's clubs. The more meetings I attended, the more amazed I became at the things that many women say and do at meetings; so much so, that I even developed into somewhat of a women's club "spy." This is what happened.

First, this book would never have been written if I had not been alphabetically elected President of my garden club while still a green new member. I knew nothing about clubs and rules and parliamentary procedure. I was not even sure how to spell the word "parliamentary," for in Georgia it is pronounced polly-mint-try.

My early married years had been spent in Australia where ladies are not so club conscious. Returning to this country with its thousands of women's organizations, I was in for many surprises. I joined possibly the only club that ever elected its officers according to their last names.

If the publicity chairman of our club had given an accurate account of the election, she might have written something like this: "At the meeting yesterday of the Tip Top Garden Club, new officers were chosen. Members whose surnames began with W, Y and Z were automatically shoved into office regardless of their willingness to serve, their ability to lead, their experience, or the length of time they had been members. The Sergeant-at-Arms was in charge of the meeting and there was no discussion."

Such a system of executive crop rotation eliminates details in parliamentary procedure, like nominating committees, voting, and counting ballots. Besides that, it does away with the excuses women offer for not holding office such as: "Since I had my gall bladder out, I keep getting funny dizzy spells," or "It makes me nervous to get up and say anything . . . gosh, I get jittery thinking about it." A favorite (next to "My daughter's having a baby in November") was "Just put me on a little ole committee, honey, just so I won't be in charge of anything."

This garden club had been clubbing along for over twenty-five years, and excuses for non-performance of duties were too thin even for retreads. Members suddenly found themselves officers according to this remarkable system, whipped up by a long-suffering member (Sweet Briar 1935) who had been re-elected President every other year.

So here was I, a new member and a confused example of the old adage, "Blessed are they who go around in circles, for they

shall be called wheels." Which way was I to turn? I was not
only the wheel but the hub cap.

The next week I heard of a dull sounding study class beginning at the YWCA called "Parliamentary Procedure for
Women's Groups Based on *Robert's Rules of Order*." I signed
up as enthusiastically as if I had dropped in at the dentist's and
suggested that he grind all my molars down to the gums just
for kicks. But I had paid my fee and it was too late to back out.

The surprise of all surprises was that the class, the teacher, the
other victims, and the textbooks were never dull—and this is a
broad statement to make about parliamentary procedure.

As our study class got underway, my husband and two sons
squirmed with disinterest as I served them warmed-over tidbits
of class activities with each helping of bacon and eggs.

"The teacher asked someone to define Privileged Motions,
and one member asked if Privileged Motions were the opposite
of Underprivileged Motions—you know, like people who are
privileged and underprivileged. Can you beat that!"

"Pass the toast, please, Daddy," Fred, Jr. interjected.

"Mom, where's my zipper jacket?" Cobby asked.

"Here we go again with the hot-and-cold-running parliamentary law, boys. Another great awakening of the middle-
aged gray matter." This was my husband's trite and repetitious
way of muttering about my ephemeral cultural pursuits. First,
there was sewing school, followed by Nurses Aide-ing, bridge
lessons, modern poetry, flower arranging, and, in later years,
book reviewing, each more temporarily enchanting than its
predecessor.

But this class, studying women's organizations and parliamentary procedure, was different. We were learning what real
women did and said at real meetings, not theory. As we took
up each section—constitutions, agenda, minutes, reports, mo-

tions, resolutions, etc.—we attended as many club meetings as
we could work into our weekly schedules as "listeners." We took
notes and read them aloud, or recorded them on tape, using
these case histories to learn the do's and do not's of conducting
meetings.

On one of my first assignments, a PTA meeting was caught
on a snag of procedure which reads, "Until a motion is seconded, there cannot be any discussion, as the motion is not yet
before the assembly."

The motion made was this: "I move that we buy heavy lined
draperies for the room where the school band practices to keep
the sound from other parts of the building, the cost not to ex-
ceed $100."

PRESIDENT: Is there a second to the motion?

FIRST MOTHER: Madame Chairman, it's ridiculous for the
PTA to spend $100 for draperies when the girl's powder room
doesn't have any good mirrors.

PRESIDENT: We have a motion on the floor and we need a
second to it.

SECOND MOTHER: Not only do they need new mirrors, but
Marjorie says they don't have enough shelves. Some girls have
to lay their books on the floor. Shelves, that's what they need!

PRESIDENT: But, ladies, first we must have a second to the
motion about the draperies.

FIRST MOTHER: (turning to member who made the motion)
Edna, you just have boys. You have no idea what a deplorable
condition the girl's powder room is in. My daughter says they
have only one tiny mirror.

PRESIDENT: (pounding the table) Please, ladies . . .

THIRD MOTHER: My little boy plays in the band and he says
the echo in the practice room is terrible and that what they
need there more than draperies is a rug.

PRESIDENT: Will the meeting please come to order again. We must get on with this motion.

FOURTH MOTHER: (raising her hand and being hopefully eyed by the president as one who would second the motion) I don't care one way or the other, because LeRoy hasn't been able to play his cornet since he had his tonsils out. I don't know if it did something to his throat or if he's being stubborn, but I paid $40 for that cornet and it's no use to anyone. Madame President, I'd like to talk with someone about getting a refund.

PRESIDENT: We will have to discuss that with the music department later, but right now, ladies, may I repeat, *we must have a second to this motion before we can have any discussion.*

FIRST MOTHER: I don't want to discuss it at all. I said I thought $100 was too much to spend on draperies when the girl's powder room needs mirrors and I still think so.

That was as far as my extraordinary notes went, but I did learn later, although no motion was seconded and no vote taken, that a determined committee of mothers installed the controversial draperies, leaving the Board of Education to come to the rescue of the powder room.

Following this PTA confabulation and several garden club horticultural discussions, I began to wonder if these womanish ramifications occur at many meetings. I soon found out. They do. And this was only the beginning of a collection of "Case Histories" of women's meetings that have been filling up pages of small black notebooks for years.

I have longed to conceal a tape recorder under a Madame Chairman's chair, but isn't there some sort of a Federal law about bugging? Unable to capture this parliamentary parlance on tape, I have substituted being an unofficial "meeting spy," and taking word-for-word shorthand notes inside of a knitting bag or a large purse. A grubby piece of half completed needle-

"YOU'VE HEARD THE MOTION
LADIES... NOW ALL THOSE
IN FAVOR SAY SOMETHING!"

point is usually cascading innocently out of the top, but note-book and ball point pen are always poised and ready for action underneath.

There was a necessity for this deceit (if that word could be applied to this harmless hobby where actual names, dates, places and faces are never recorded, and likewise are lost in the limbo of meetings and more meetings). At first I made the mistake of asking permission from the chairman and members to jot down notes on the meetings, explaining in good faith that in studying and teaching parliamentary procedure I needed some candid chatter to use for comparisons. The answer was always the same—shrieks of protest.

Here my own hieroglyphic shorthand has proved its worth. This hen-scratching original mumbo-jumbo is a legacy from days as a newspaper writer, and I will wager it against any speedy Munson or Gregg shorthand system. The only disadvantage is that these scribblings must be decoded before they get cold. A memorandum like "Ms Mayb rs 2 pt ord wh mt dcl adj" cannot wait too long to be recorded in long hand, for it would be easy to forget that Mrs. Mabrey rose to a point of order when the meeting was declared adjourned.

My conscience remains clear and unclouded, however, for when I have returned these little "bungles" to a group so as to assist them in learning some basic rules of law and order, I have yet to encounter a single case of hostility. Women love to laugh at themselves, and especially at their friends.

One of the first "bloopers" on record in that initial little black book was when a portly Madame Chairman pounded the table with her gavel while a motion was being tossed about and made this exceptional proclamation: "Ladies, we have a motion on the floor, and it has been seconded, and we are ready to vote. *All those in favor say something!*"

So, all of my spy notes actually are only concerned with the non-conformist, the unpredictable, and the un-everything member. So, if you are a woman, and if you belong to any woman's organization, you know that you have never been guilty of any of this twiddle-twaddle. I am speaking of someone else, my dear, not you.

Mass Hypnotism

When our study classes were over, the mature graduates departed from the ivied halls of the YWCA armed with esoteric data to enlighten the world of women's clubs. My collection of wrong ways to conduct or participate in meetings was now relegated to the rear of my notebook in the "You'd-Never-Believe-It" section, as we now were concentrating only on very correct procedure.

The society editor wrote about us in her "Chit-Chat" column:

> "Members of women's clubs in Augusta and surrounding areas in Georgia and South Carolina will be interested to learn that the first class of trainees in the YWCA Adult Education classes in Parliamentary Law have completed their courses as of yesterday. These ladies, many of them prominent in local women's organizations, are now ready to share their knowledge as volunteer speakers or teachers. Program chairmen are asked to phone the Y, and one of these ladies will be happy to give a program or teach a series of classes. Speakers will be assigned on a first-come,

first-served basis, so, club chairmen, set up your dates as soon as possible."

So, here we were, poised and ready, anticipating the onslaught of invitations from those myriads of club ladies athirst for knowledge. We discussed among our learned selves how best we could share this wisdom without some sacrifice on the home front.

We waited, and then we waited a while longer. Finally it became a habit to wait. Our readiness was akin to being on a ship and preparing for a hurricane which turned and went in the other direction. Our hatches were battened down, mainsails were taut, life belts on . . . and we found ourselves floating on a quiet mill pond of indifference. It became apparent that ladies evidently liked the sloppy manner in which their business was conducted, and they preferred to run their silly old clubs their own way. As if we cared!

Weeks went by, and parliamentary law classes were forgotten during a flurry of redecorating and bulb planting. More and more publicity appeared about the available speakers, and I strongly suspect prodding and taunting in the background from higher-ups in club echelons, for the requests slowly began to dribble in. Some of those nice club ladies did want us all the time; they just had not gotten around to inviting us, bless their hearts.

My first invitation to teach parliamentary law did not strongly suggest a club craving much enlightenment. It read:

Dear Mrs. Ware:

We have had a letter from our state chairman insisting that we start our year off with a study of parliamentary procedure if we are to receive national rating. We called the YWCA and they gave us your name as the only speaker available.

Our meeting will be at 4 o'clock on Thursday and we are hoping to learn all about Robert's Rules of Order, and how to conduct our business meetings in an orderly way, how to make motions, vote, and all the other things you do at meetings. We will be looking forward to having you as our speaker.

Sincerely,

B———— G————

P.S. We usually allot at least 15 minutes for our program.

Unless a speaker has the gift to quack as fast as Donald Duck, it is quite a feat to condense a twelve-week study into a quarter of an hour. Maybe I should have abandoned the whole thing, but I had read too many magazine articles about aging matrons going to pot. Having acquired this pedagogical status, I resolved to gird up the loins of my mind and charge . . . even if I had to do it in fifteen minutes.

A gentleman fellow parliamentarian who learned his rules from the famous Toastmasters International, Inc. vows that this also happened to him. The presiding Madame Chairman announced to the membership, "Our speaker today is going to teach us all about Robert's Rules of Order in the ten minutes we have before lunch."

Not only do these ladies who yearn to learn the rules often appear bored with the whole idea, but I made another amazing discovery. Parliamentary law has the same effect on an audience as mass hypnotism. It is equally as effective as hearing Professor VooDoo repeat in a monotone that everyone is getting sleepier and sleepier as the magic pendulum swings back and forth, back and forth.

" OUR SPEAKER TODAY IS GOING TO TEACH US ALL ABOUT ROBERT'S RULES OF ORDER IN THE TEN MINUTES WE HAVE BEFORE LUNCH SO LISTEN CAREFULLY..!"

As the months went by, and more and more organizations halfheartedly requested this program or a more prolonged study class, the results were the same. A cloud of gloom seemed to float in with the audience. There was poor attendance, and my closest friends would wink and say, "I hear you're teaching parliamentary law to our club today. Well, I'll be sure and not get there until time for the luncheon. Ha Ha Ha!"

During the lectures there were always the inveterate chair shifters, the ceiling watchers, the wrist watch glancers, the chain smokers, the leg crossers, the yawners, and the eyelid droopers. Sometimes, in a warm, comfortable room with an audience of more "settled ladies," there would start the heaving of the bosoms, a deep-breathing routine, as weighty eyelids ceased to flutter and chins rested comfortably on other chins.

It is difficult enough for one with a corn-fed Georgia accent to pay careful attention to cor-rect e-nun-ci-a-tion, and to concentrate on such sage doctrine as "provisions deemed advisable in by-laws whereby, whereas, and wherefore are fundamental parliamentary principles that can be transacted as either pro or con." But to do this and keep an audience awake long enough to teach them anything about parliamentary procedure was a problem.

I recalled with nostalgia the beloved minister of our Presbyterian Church in Atlanta. He had a soft, soothing voice, and on many a warm summer Sunday morning I can remember his startling the communicants from their slumbers by booming every few minutes, "AND THE LORD SAID!" I attempted to duplicate this on a minor scale by banging on the table with an ash tray and braying something about what the rule book said, but it was ineffectual. The sleepers would stir for a fleeting moment, but that was about all.

Once in a large meeting in a woman's club in South Caro-

"MADAME CHAIRMAN, I MOVE THAT WE SPEND THE CLUB DEFICIT ON FLOWERS FOR OUR STATE PRESIDENT WHO IS IN THE HOSPITAL."

lina following a sumptuous four-course luncheon, I began to get desperate. Several members on the front row had gone past the deep breathing exercises and were resorting to audible nasal wheezing. I suddenly recalled my "spy notes" collection in the back of the loose leaf notebook I used as parliamentary guide, and an idea was born.

"Today, ladies," I announced frantically, "I'm going to reverse our program. Instead of telling you *how* to run your meetings, I shall share with you some of my secret notes on *how not* to run your meetings." I opened my notebook and my eyes fell on "Notes on Treasurers' Reports":

"The meeting had been a statewide conference of church women, and various districts were giving their reports. The day was warm, and voices droned on with monotonous regularity and routine reports. Then, a bit of excitement was in the air. District Two, of all things, regretted to report that they had a deficit of $10.64 in their treasury. Before the chairman could comment on this unhappy state of affairs, a young woman bobbed up enthusiastically and waved her hand to be recognized by the chair. 'Madame Chairman,' she called out, 'I'd like to make a motion that we spend the deficit on flowers for our district chairman who's in the hospital.' The motion was seconded quickly by an equally enthusiastic member, before the surprised chairman could even reach for her gavel, much less bang for order."

This had a tendency to rouse some of the members from their slumber. Next I told them about the new PTA chairman who called her first meeting to order, then smiled at the equally new and inexperienced secretary and said, "We will now have the reading of the moments."

Then I mentioned the secretary in a South Carolina city who served in the same capacity for two organizations. She read the minutes of the other club, but in the confusion of late arrivals, no one seemed to notice. She discovered her own mistake when she began to read the same minutes to the correct club the following day.

My newly awakened audience was charmed to hear about the garden club from the small Georgia town that attempted to file their new club's name at the state convention. A more discreet name was suggested by the executive committee when it was discovered that they had chosen to call themselves, "The Weeders and Ho'ers" Garden Club.

Everyone became suddenly awake, alert, interested and even anxious to hear more about parliamentary law and what goes on at club meetings—the wrong way, that is. Let's see how things progressed after this discovery.

Among My Souvenirs

Why do women suddenly give birth to ideas, notions, pet peeves, schemes, suggestions, projects, plans, and even inventions, when they attend any meeting where *let's do something* strategy is being hatched?

As soon as the idea ball begins to roll on the playing field of *big plans*, most women will grab it between their teeth and run like seasoned halfbacks. They are not heading for any particular goal, but just around and around the field until some more glib contender takes over.

Amidst this gravity there is little levity. It is serious business when "Virginia wants to order the cupcakes from the bakery and that will cost at least $14. I figure we can make them at home for about $7. I've already checked the whole thing, girls, and we can make them out of two large boxes of cake mix. Now, cake mix will be 37 cents more than the plain flour, but it has all the stuff in it except the milk and eggs. But keep this in mind, that does not include the chocolate for the icing. I thought we could all do that at our own expense."

There is a certain satisfaction in this collective economy, and the ladies feel quite shrewd when they beat the neighborhood

"THE BIG PROBLEM FACING US IS WHETHER TO SPEND $14 FOR CUP CAKES, OR TO MAKE THEM OURSELVES AND KEEP OUR TREASURY STABLE FOR THE REST OF THE MONTH."

bakery out of a small profit, and help the wavering treasury to hold together precariously for another week.

No consideration is given to the fact that this frugality involved three trips to the supermarket, ten telephone calls, plus a twenty mile pick-up drive around sparsely settled suburbs, not to mention a few ruffled feathers because "some of the cup cakes didn't have enough icing on them, and Rose had to ice them all over after we got back to the church."

———

Once as the guest speaker at a garden club meeting, I was quietly working in the far corner of the living room in preparation for a demonstration on flower arrangements. The card table which was to serve as my exhibition stand was covered with a table cloth reaching to the floor. As I lifted flowers and vases from the floor to the table, I could duck behind the cloth and scribble unobserved, jotting notes to take back to our study group. (Pre-knitting bag days.)

This was the club's annual report meeting, and a disconcerted president was searching through her notes for some elusive papers. She flipped pages, and occasionally would hold her notebook aloft and loose sheets would drift hither and yon. She was calling upon a lengthy list of chairmen for annual reports, while she and her secretary continued to rummage through reams of papers for a missing something.

The reports were in order, dull, and well executed. I scratched along in my little notebook unobserved, and listened attentively for some blunder. Then the president called for the project chairman's report.

PROJECT CHAIRMAN: There was *something* the garden club was supposed to do before April. Does anybody remember what it was? . . . (Silence) . . . I had so much company last month during the Masters Tournament that I had to clean out all of those drawers in the chest in the guest room where I keep my garden club books. Well . . . Can't somebody remember what our project was for the year? (Silence again. Madame President did not come to the rescue, for by that time she and the Secretary had their flowered hats practically entwined, as they continued to jiggle their notebooks and paw through their handbags, as they conferred on what seemed to be highly confidential matters.)

INTERESTED MEMBER: Is that the chest Mr. Swatz did over for you?

PROJECT CHAIRMAN (still standing): Yes, and he made a grand job of it too.

INTERESTED MEMBER: What kind of wood was it when he got that black paint scraped off? Was it pine?

PROJECT CHAIRMAN: No, it was walnut, but it has such a light finish that it goes grand with that spool bed Mama gave me.

(Here began a soft buzz. A number of members nodded their heads and confirmed the fact that, yes indeed, they *did* remember the spool bed that had belonged to Mama, and one and all agreed that the old chest had definitely needed doing over for years.)

PROJECT CHAIRMAN: Walnut and pine look much alike if they are finished the same light color, don't you think so? (The members nodded in agreement.)

(At this point the president stood, smiled at the group, removed her glasses, rapped the gavel and continued with the business at hand.)

PRESIDENT: Thank you very much. Now, you've all heard the

eport of the project chairman. Next we'll hear from our pub-
icity chairman.

The welcoming speech to some 200 women attending a dis-
rict church conference in a small town near Augusta will long
)e remembered by many delegates. It was a bitter cold and
windy day, and many of the women had braved the elements
it 6 a.m. to make the long drive before the 9 o'clock session be-
;an. The ladies swarmed into the sanctuary and were greeted
)y a charming, gray-haired president, grandmotherly in pale
avender wool with flowered felt hat to match. Her voice rang
)ut cordially:

"I am happy to welcome you ladies from so many towns to
Westernboro. We have a wonderful program planned for the
lay. Before we begin the meeting, we would like to invite all of
'ou into the church parlors here at my right for some hot coffee
o warm you up on this cold morning.

"Oh, and another announcement: during the freeze yester-
lay the water pipes in the church froze, and the plumber hasn't
)een able to get here to fix them. He said he thought the meet-
ng was tomorrow, and because so many other people's pipes are
frozen he couldn't get here—at least that's what he claimed.
Anyway, the ladies' room is disconnected . . . you know . . .
10 running water.

"But we have arranged everything beautifully with the Fire
Department across the street. Right after the coffee break, if
iny of you ladies want to powder your noses, go out this side
loor here on my left, across the street, and down to that corner
o the Fire Department. It's right there on that first corner . . .
hat red brick building. The firemen will be expecting you.

"And I would like to say that we are indeed grateful to Chie: McKewon for this courtesy, and while I'm thinking of it I wan to ask the Corresponding Secretary if she would write a littl note to our nice Chief on behalf of the Women of the Churcl to thank those kind firemen for their generosity in sharin their conveniences with us on this happy occasion."

———

One of the least enlightening of all discussions I ever re corded word-for-word was filed under the heading "Paintin vs. Tuning vs. Painting," with a nice lived-happily-ever-afte ending. It went like this:

CHAIRMAN: Well, that about winds up the business for to day. Will someone make a motion that the meeting be ad journed?

NELL: What about the piano?

CHAIRMAN: Oh, yes, maybe we should mention that, but didn't think it was important enough to bring before the entir group because it isn't going to cost but $10.

WINNIE: What's not going to cost but $10? Are we going t have the piano tuned? I know a man who will tune it for $7, i I can think of his name.

CHAIRMAN: No, we're going to have it painted, not tuned Some of the ladies thought we might have the piano painte blue.

WINNIE: But I think it sounds tinny. Let's have it tuned That man won't charge but $7.

CHAIRMAN: No, we haven't talked about having it tuned just painted.

WINNIE: If we plan to have any Christmas music, I think i needs tuning. I remember the man's name now. It's Mr. Boaz man or Bazemore.

"— SO WHEN WE GET A MOTION ON THE FLOOR THAT MEANS WE HAVE TO DO SOMETHING ABOUT IT."

CHAIRMAN: Well, suppose we appoint a committee to look into these suggestions.

NELL: We've already looked into it, and Edna's husband isn't charging us anything except for the paint. He's sending a man out from the store to do it.

CHAIRMAN: Louise, will you be in charge of the committee to get this settled about the piano?

LOUISE: What are we going to settle? I thought you all had decided to have it painted. Anyway, I think I have done my part this year about trying to get up committees and prodding people to come to meetings. Let somebody else be chairman . . . or better still, why don't we put this thing in the form of a motion. I've got to take my child to ballet at 4 o'clock.

CHAIRMAN: That's a good idea. It's almost 4 o'clock now. Everybody pay attention, please, we're getting ready to have a motion on the floor and when we get something on the floor that means we have to do something about it, and we will have to vote before we leave.

NELL: All right, now, here I go. Madame Chairman, I make a motion that we have the piano painted blue to match the rugs and draperies—a soft blue, that is—and spend only $10 for the paint.

CHAIRMAN: Is there a second to the motion? Thank you. Any discussion? Those in favor say aye; those opposed, no. Well, that seems to be unanimous. Wait a minute . . . Winnie says the piano still sounds tinny to her and that the piano tuner's name is Brazemon, and he lives on Sand Bar Ferry Road. She looked it up in the phone book. Well, I guess that is about all the business today. I wish we'd thought of putting this thing in a motion to begin with and we'd have been through. That's all, girls. The meeting is finally adjourned."

Call Me Madame President

To be elected president or chairman is, of course, the highest honor a group can bestow upon one of its members. The club women's booklets stress that when one is chosen for this high office, the president "should accept with graciousness, enthusiasm, and a positive attitude, resolving in every way to cooperate with the group and be appreciative of such devotion, respect and esteem."

Following one organization's election of officers, the caption under the newspaper photograph reported that a "distinct honor was bestowed on a local club leader yesterday, when Mrs. Fason Jason was unanimously elected District President of the Children's Benevolent Association at the State Conference in Macon. Mrs. Jason, shown above graciously accepting the gavel, said that she considered it a distinct privilege and a great opportunity to serve."

As a member of the Nominating Committee who coerced gracious little Mrs. Jason into accepting this high honor I had this to report in my notes.

MRS. JASON: You are wasting your time coming to see me about being President. If you want to know the truth, I'm so sick of the whole group I could scream.

COMMITTEE MEMBER: But, my dear Mrs. Jason, you've done such a wonderful job as Vice-President, and now you deserve the honor of being the President. No one could possibly take over the Presidency like you could.

MRS. JASON: No one but a moron who was willing to work like a horse. I just wish you all knew the things those women backed out on last spring when we were putting on that building fund drive.

COMMITTEE MEMBER: Well, now, my dear . . . let's don't recall all that now because it *did* turn out all right after all, you know.

MRS. JASON: I'll say it did, but you know who finished it, don't you? I had to take over and reorganize the whole thing. I bet I could write a book about Standing Committees that don't stand. You should hear my husband . . . why, the very mention of the Children's Benevolent Association and he goes *wild!*

COMMITTEE CHAIRMAN (the gentle-persuader type with years of experience): But, now, my dear, let me explain it to you. You see, as President, you really won't have all that responsibility this year. Everyone will help you. It will be like this . . .

Old-hand Nominating Committees refer to this portion of an unrecorded and highly confidential confab with a weakening prospect as the "coup de grace," but this has long been forgotten, and most of us believe what we read in the papers anyway.

———

There was one Madame Chairman I knew who was conducting a noisy meeting of a committee of the local music association. Finally, she managed to get everyone's attention by banging on the table with an ash tray, always an excellent substitute for a gavel.

"All right now ladies. Please, may I have your attention. We *must* come to some decision today about whether we are going to have the reception after the concert. We've already had two motions on the floor and nobody has seconded either of them. I'm beginning to think maybe you don't want to bother with this thing."

————————

The vice-president, of course, is expected to preside in the absence of the president, and generally she accomplishes this with acumen and poise that would befit a well-trained "stand-in" for a Broadway actress. However, when I attended a meeting where the president was absent and took down the vice-president's words verbatim, they went this way:

VICE-PRESIDENT: I know you all are wondering why I'm up here presiding today instead of Mary, but she had to change her beauty parlor appointment, and this was the only day her beauty operator could give her a permanent. She was real sorry about the way things turned out, but she couldn't help it. Friday is her regular day, but the beauty operator says that Friday is too busy a day to give a permanent, and this morning she called Mary and said she had a cancellation and for her to come right away. I'm sure everybody will understand, because her son is getting married in Atlanta next month, and she and Bill are going up there this week end to visit the new in-laws and Mary said her hair looked a sight. She really didn't want to have the permanent until next week, but, then she didn't want to wait too long because her hair might be too kinky, and she wants it to look especially good for the wedding. Then, too, she was afraid if she didn't take this appointment when she could get it, she might miss out on having this regular girl to give her a permanent, because she's taking her vacation in about a week . . . the beauty operator, not Mary . . . and this girl is the only one who can make Mary's hair stay curled. She uses that new high-style spray lotion, and it is most becoming to her that way —piled up high in front, you know, and sort of swooped in the back this way. So, she brought these things by my house this morning. Actually, I haven't had time to go over them, but Mary said she had everything written down in the agenda, and if everybody will sit down now, I'd like to call the meeting to order.

PRESIDENT: Now, will someone please put this in the form of a motion that we invite these two people as special guests.

MEMBER: Madame Chairman, I made that motion about 10 minutes ago, and it has been seconded and voted upon.

PRESIDENT: Well, what do you know. That must have happened while we were serving coffee. Now . . . what's next on the agenda?

Every women's club has a favorite tale they like to tell. One organization, which is the proud possessor of their own headquarters building, built an ecclesiastical looking podium in their assembly room, and the president suddenly developed a phobia about presiding from that elevation.

"I don't know what has happened to me," she confided to a fellow member. "I not only have stage fright but all the time I am up there I have a strange feeling that my husband is hiding under the chair telling me what to do. It has become such an obsession with me," and she lowered her voice to a whisper, "that I am going tomorrow to consult a psychiatrist."

A few days later her friend passed her on the street and they paused to chat. "Tell me, my dear," the friend inquired, "what did the psychiatrist advise you to do?"

"Well, actually I didn't go, and I'm glad because everything has worked out beautifully. I was telling someone else about my problem, and she gave me Dr. Norman Vincent Peale's book, 'The Power of Positive Thinking,' so I just had the legs sawed off the chair, and everything is wonderful now!"

Or what about the president who had this to say: "The program chairman wants us to vote on whether to continue our study on 'Wild flowers in America' this year, or whether we should update our programs with the study suggested in our national magazine, 'Psychedelic Phenomena in Mass Botanical Culture.' Personally, I think we should keep on concentrating on the wild flowers, because everything is confusing enough these days."

CHAIRMAN: We chose the new members by secret ballot and I'm happy to announce that the decision was unanimous, with the exception of two votes.

Treasurers and High Finance

Finance, too, has a way of entering into the perplexities of a woman's club world. Consider, for instance, some of the treasurers' reports I have taken down word-for-word. One treasurer I knew even wanted to keep her report a secret.

PRESIDENT: We will now have the Treasurer's report.

TREASURER: No report, Madame Chairman.

PRESIDENT: But surely you must have some report to make.

TREASURER: I can't give any report because we haven't any money in the treasury.

PRESIDENT: But don't you have a record of what you have spent? It is a report, you know, even if we don't have any money.

TREASURER: It's even worse than that. We are minus something! I just hated to bring it up at our spring luncheon.

———————

Some young and inexperienced club officers are not sufficiently adept at club strategy to realize the importance of never admitting errors. This girl was ready for the confessional even before she was accused:

TREASURER: I am sorry that I made a mistake in my Treasurer's report last month. I added something that I should have subtracted, and it got in the wrong line of figures. Instead of having $24.00 in the treasury, we are minus $2.40. Madame Chairman, my husband thinks maybe I had better resign as Treasurer . . . but I would be glad to swap jobs with someone . . . because I don't want you to think I'm not doing my part.

Some more experienced keepers of the funds are not as apologetic or as subtle concerning financial situations. At a business women's club in a hotel private dining room, I managed to jot down the exact words of one custodian as she strolled around the table collecting from each member and making businesslike scribblings on the back of the menu card:

TREASURER: Everyone listen, now. Our dinners were $2.75 each, and everybody is supposed to put in a quarter for the tip. That comes to $3.00 each. No, Mrs. Ware, you are our guest and you are not to pay. Wait a minute now, and let me figure this out. There are 17 of us. Mrs. Ware's dinner and tip will be $3.00, and $3.00 divided by 17 . . . I think that makes it about $17\frac{1}{2}$ cents each. Isn't that right, Christine? Add it up . . . Christine says it doesn't work out right at $17\frac{1}{2}$ cents, and nobody has any pennies. So, let's do this. Suppose we put in 20 cents each for Mrs. Ware's dinner, and we will give that extra to the waiter. We've had such good service here tonight. Is that O.K. with everyone?

From a club financial report:
"After a rather lively discussion, the club members voted not to include their ages on the typed forms the treasurer filled out

for state headquarters. It was decided that under 'date of birth,' we write something more dignified like 'well after the turn of the century.' "

———————

That envoy of good will, the banker, who deals adroitly with lady club treasurers, also fits into the women's club picture. Let me cite an example:

TREASURER: Some people haven't paid their dues. I don't have the treasurer's book with me today. I was going to be gone all day and I didn't think we had enough money in the bank to warrant my lugging that big check book around during this Christmas rush. I do have the bank statement, though, but it doesn't balance with mine.

Now here is what I thought we might do. If everyone will pay their dues today, maybe I could work something out. According to my records we are supposed to have somewhere around $8 or $9 in the treasury. I talked to that nice man at the bank. I don't know his name, but he sits at the first desk on the right . . . has sorta dark hair. Well, anyway, he was so polite and understanding about it that I didn't want to get into an argument. I told him about the dues not all being paid up, and that maybe I had some names down as paid when they had just thought they had paid. I figured I'd better check up today and see because that man at the bank . . . he couldn't have been any nicer . . . he told me to get all the names of the members who had paid and he'd be glad to go over the books and help me straighten it out. He said the bank has all sorts of services and they'd be glad to help us with any problems . . . but that they couldn't do much if we actually didn't have the money.

———————

Ladies also have a nimble way of taking advantage of every opportunity, especially when they "have the floor," a position not always easy to attain or retain. At one PTA meeting the president had inquired if the budget committee had completed the year's budget and would care to report. The budget chairman rose:

"Madame President, we have not completed the budget yet and plan to have another meeting here at the school tomorrow with the lunchroom chairman before we make our report. But while I have the floor, I would like to ask if there is anyone here who lives in Westwick or Murray Hills who would like to be in a second grade car pool on Tuesdays? If so, please see me after the meeting, or call REgent 3-4098."

There are some women who seem to have a natural flair for sharing details, even when the occasion calls for something as unexceptional as resigning an office. One treasurer's resignation went like this:

"Madame Chairman, I will give my report today, but after next month someone may have to take my job because there is a possibility that George may be transferred. We are not sure yet, but we should know something definite by next week.

"You know that cute house up on the corner of Rock Springs Road, the one with the sort of gray picket fence and the big stone chimney? Well, we were up there again Sunday looking at that house, and the real estate man came by and we came within an inch of making the man an offer right then. I sure am glad we didn't, because we could be transferred by next month, although it isn't settled yet. That would have been a mess, after renting all these years.

"Sara, hand me that black book there on the floor next to my bag . . . thanks . . . well, the way I figure it, we've got some-where around $28 in the treasury, but all the bills are not in for this month and I haven't added up what we took in today. To tell you the truth, I've been so upset over the possibility of our making this move and taking the children out of school right in the middle of the year that I haven't had good sense.

"Let me see now . . . $28.19. Don't write that down in the minutes, Catherine, because I haven't added last month's dues and haven't checked the bills. We should be able to tell some-thing by next week. George is in Atlanta now, and as soon as we find out, I'll check this all up and give it to whoever takes over my job . . . that is, if we are transferred and I have to re-sign. That's the thing about these big companies . . ."

———

Another time there was the Ways and Means Chairman with a watchful eye on future expenditures. Proposals were be-ing discussed for the garden club's part in the city-wide beau-tification plan which in this case was a downtown park sector. The weighty problem was being analyzed with the solemnity of a world court in session. The Project Chairman rose to the occasion with this proposal:

"We put $30 worth of fertilizer on our downtown garden plot last year, and everything grew so fast it cost us $5 a month extra to pay Annie's yard man to keep going down there to prune everything. I would like to suggest that this year we only put $15 worth of fertilizer on it. Would anyone like to put that in the form of a motion?"

———

In Augusta garden club circles if mention is made of unor-thodox bookkeeping for club treasurers, someone will surely

ll you the story of Anna and the pearl pin. Like many house-
ives, Anna operates on a budget. Once when that budget was
retched to the breaking point and a bargain loomed upon
ie horizon . . . well, this is the way she explained it at the
lub meeting when she gave her treasurer's report:

"Madame Chairman, I would like to offer an explanation
ith my report that we have no money in the treasury. Some of
ou might wonder what became of the $40 we had at the last
ieeting. Here's what happened, and I believe after I explain it
hat you will agree that I couldn't have done otherwise. To put
: bluntly, I spent the money for this pearl pin. See how well it
uits this green dress and looks even better on brown.

"Here's how it happened. Cullum's was having a sale, and
his pin was marked down to half price—exactly $40. I was on
ny way to the bank when I happened to pass through the store,
o I hope you understand that I didn't plan it deliberately. I had
he $40 stuffed in the top of my bag, and when I opened the zip-
er, it practically flew up at me.

"So I began to think about it and came up with this wonder-
ul idea. This is our last meeting until October so that leaves
uly, August and September with that money lying up there in
ur club checking account not doing anybody any good. I got
ut my pencil and figured it on a businesslike basis. I divided
40 by the 13 weeks until our next meeting, and it came to a
ittle over $3 a week. I could buy the pin, take $3 a week of my
rocery allowance, and by October the club will have the full
mount in the bank, and I could have my beautiful pin at half
rice. Another advantage is that I wouldn't have to put it on
ny charge account and have my husband ask me if I'd lost my
eeble mind paying $40 for a piece of costume jewelry.

"Is that all right with everybody? You don't blame me? Well, thanks, girls, I feel better about the whole affair now. And by the way, the sale is going on all week in case you're interested."

———

At one meeting when the secretary was reading the minutes from the previous month, this was her complete report on the financial condition of the club: "At the November meeting letter from the bank was read by the treasurer, stating that our account was overdrawn by $8.12. Mrs. Raine made a motion that this letter be received as information. The motion was seconded and passed."

Secretaries Have Their Moments

That little woman who suggested that "we will now have the reading of the moments," might have had a point. A club secretary does spend many moments on her notes if she does an efficient job, and not a moment at the meeting can be missed, as she must be on the alert to keep an accurate record—more of what is done at the meeting than what is said.

Sometimes she jots down every word, and if the notes are not edited and rewritten before they are read . . . well . . . things like this happen: "At the December meeting of the Woman's Club someone suggested that we have a discussion about Red China, but one of the ladies opposed this because she said it would look all right for our Christmas party, but she felt plain white china would be more practical for year-round use in the club dining room."

———————

Another secretary had in her notes: "In a discussion at the last meeting of members' qualifications for having their names put on the ballot for state president, the chairman said that since Mrs. Hayden had caught the largest blue fin tuna caught off

the coast of Florida last winter, in competition with the mer
that Mrs. Hayden was well qualified to take on such a job a
state president."

———————

Occasionally some bizarre circumstances pop up in the min
utes.

SECRETARY: Madame Chairman, there's a reason why I can
read the club minutes today, and I am going to need some hel
in trying to straighten this situation out. Our secretary's boo
has sprung a leak.

That sounds strange, and I'll explain. This book . . . se
right here . . . well, where this torn place is in the canva
cover is where it's leaking. I've had it in the trunk of my car dur
ing all of this rain, and I didn't know it had gotten wet until
turned it up this way . . . look everybody, you can see the wa
ter dripping right out of the cover. Everything has all run to
gether and the ink is so blurred I can't see to read it. What d
you think I should do?

PRESIDENT: Well, this is an unusual situation that hasn
come up before while I've been president. Does anyone know
if we have any rules or by-laws to take care of a case like this
Not too many secretaries have their books spring a leak.

MEMBER: Madame Chairman, I have an idea. Why don'
we vote to dispense with the reading of the minutes until the
dry out next month, and if we still can't read them, we'll buy a
new waterproof book and begin all over again. I'll put that in
the form of a motion if everyone agrees.

———————

A club secretary of great ingenuity and foresight is my frien
Jane, who has capably headed up more than her share of civi

drives and projects with the aplomb of a lady judge. As a guest at her garden club, I learned from her own lips a new term in parliamentary law: "to basket."

SECRETARY: Here's a letter from the Better Betterment League asking for another contribution. Madame President, does the club want to shelve this request for the present or basket it?

PRESIDENT: Jane, I know what it means to shelve something, but I don't understand what you mean by *basket* it. Will you explain that to the group, please?

SECRETARY: In this club we get so many requests that we always vote to shelve them. That means that we put them in this folder in the back of the Secretary's book. We seldom get around to looking at them again, because by the next meeting we get more letters. Actually, all it does is to clutter up the Secretary's book . . . see, how this thing bulges. Now, when we vote to *basket* it, I read the letter, and unless we vote to do something about it at that meeting I lean over like this . . . see . . . and drop it in the trash basket. Actually, it amounts to the same thing, but there is less clutter and it does away with that big lump in the back cover. Don't forget that I have been Secretary of this club twice before, and I know that is the only way we can solve what I call the Club Accumulation Problem. It is just an idea, but I'm sure it will work out fine. Do I make myself clear now, Madame President?

―――――――

Sometimes minutes are scratched off hurriedly at a business session and cannot be carefully and legibly transcribed into the Secretary's official notebook. One old envelope folded into a wallet revealed these interesting facts: "At the November meeting it was voted . . . no, it wasn't voted on, just talked about, I think it says here . . . that our club would send two delegates to the state convention. No, let me see if I can make this out . . . It says we appointed the two delegates but it looks like they are to go on their own expense if they decide to go. There's something here about funds, or maybe it says no funds. I seem to remember that we didn't have enough money to send but one delegate, but we had appointed two before we checked up. Does anyone remember exactly how that went? I didn't have my secretary's book with me last month, and this has sorta faded out, so I can't read it very well. . . ."

Once when a garden club secretary took off on a flying tour of European gardens, the whereabouts of the official club record book was unknown. A pinch-hitting secretary who jotted down the minutes on a piece of scratch paper possibly had intentions of copying her notes before they were turned in to be recorded, but, alas, "a little neglect may breed mischief," for at the next meeting they were read as written:

"At the May meeting of the Garden Club, plans were made for a flower show to be held in October. Don't forget dry cleaning, laundry, eggs, bread, milk, mustard, hamburger, dog food, and get oil changed in car. The minutes were read and approved, and the treasurer reported that all bills are paid through April, and the treasury shows a balance of $17.81."

The chairman of a large civic organization was an experienced and exacting expediter, but the secretary taking over her first role in public office was having problems with her ball point pen. As the speaker, I was seated next to her, so it was easy to capture and scribble every word she spoke or whispered

s she attempted to overcome the difficulties of a pen that re-
used to function.

SECRETARY: Madame Chairman, don't let anybody say any-
hing until I can get this pen to write. There's a knob here I'm
upposed to punch but the little do-jigger won't stay down. It's
vorking now, so let's start. Will everybody please repeat what
hey have said and not talk too fast. I told you'all when I took
his job that I can't take shorthand.

CHAIRMAN: Edna, you don't have to take every word that is
poken. Only the gist of the business needs to be in the minutes.

SECRETARY: But if the people talk too fast I don't know
vhat to write down or leave out. Mildred not only talks fast
ut she runs her words together. All right, I'm ready.

CHAIRMAN: We have a motion on the floor; do I hear a second?

SECRETARY: What was the motion?

CHAIRMAN: Would you mind repeating the motion, please.
The secretary didn't understand it.

SECRETARY: I'm really paying attention, ladies, even if I am
having trouble with my pen, but the blower fan makes so much
noise that we can't hear in the front.

CHAIRMAN: The motion has been seconded and passed, but
he secretary has requested that someone loan her a pen or pencil or she says she'll never get this in the minutes. Never mind.
She says this was her old pen that needed a new filler, and she
had the new one in her bag all the time. Coffee break, everybody.

More gleanings from secretary's minutes:

"At the Retired Officers' Club meeting Saturday evening, the
business meeting was not completed. The chairman said that

following the interruption for the serving of cocktails tha
things never seemed to get going again."

"The Poetry Study Club's membership has dropped so dras-
tically during the past three years that it was decided at the
May meeting to discontinue the study of modern poets, and
substitute bridge for the next six months."

"Several members of the Hill Top Garden Club spent Tuesday in Atlanta attending the School of Landscape Design.
There were no reports brought back to the club, however, as
the members only attended one session due to Rich's Harvest
Sale which was in progress the same day."

"A correction was made in the minutes following an objec-
tion from the club pianist, Mrs. McKinney. She said that at the
March meeting, song number 78, 'Oh How Lovely the Spring'
was sung, instead of song number 87, 'A Lovely Day is Dawn-
ing for Us All,' as was reported by the secretary."

"There were so many controversial subjects on the agenda
that the board members decided to dispense with the business
and show the color films we took at the spring picnic."

"For the March meeting of the PTA the planned program
was for fathers of the seventh grade students to do an amusing
skit in ballet costumes. Unfortunately, so many of the fathers

had to work that evening, or were out of town, that the skit was called off. The Choral Society substituted with a delightful musical program."

_____

"The secretary was instructed to write to the State Bulletin asking that the state award won by the Happy Garden Club be re-lettered, as the club was mistakenly referred to as the 'Hippy Club.' When this takes place, the award will then be framed and hung in the Garden Center."

_____

"The Health committee suggested that a Jogging Club be organized during the summer months. No one put this in the form of a motion so the idea was shelved until September."

_____

"The Thursday Book Club voted not to review any books next year that deal with student revolts, race riots, politics, sex, marchers, the pill, poverty programs, war, or L.S.D. To date the program committee has not decided on but one book, 'Native Birds of Arizona.' "

_____

"The day lilies we planted around the Court House all died for the third straight year. The club voted to replant the lilies, also to adopt as our club slogan, 'Dream the Impossible Dream.' "

Program Chairmen

In every club there is always at least one of those efficient members, the conscientious and the old reliable. Ours happens to be Radmore, Class of 1932, with the English tweeds, the sensible hair cut and the serviceable flats. There is never cause to question the judgment of good ole dependable, trustworthy Gertrude. She does her little chores with perfection, and when it comes her time to serve as program chairman, she always shows up with a gem.

On one occasion, though, Gertrude outdid herself. She routed out a former roommate's husband who had been hovering in the background at the class reunion the previous spring, and had him well in tow to perform at one of our winter meetings. We were fortunate, because he was a nationally known figure, we were told. Gertrude glibly called him an "insecticidian," an eminent professor who not only wrote books but got them published. He knew everything there was to know about bug killing and spraying. The roommate and her insecticidic spouse had been invited to Augusta for a visit en route to Florida. ("Honey, we're right on Highway One. You have to come smack dab through Augusta to drive to Florida from where you live," we are certain Gertrude told them, for that is the local stock phrase used to lure nice Yankee friends for visits.)

It was such an auspicious occasion that our club decided to share with other associations this illustrious dignitary who knew about killer bugs, one of our most serious warm-climate problems. His importance and national standing increased each time Florence, our garden page editor and fellow member, got him going between her typewriter ribbon and keys. The event gathered momentum and promised to be a city-wide project at the Garden Center, with hundreds of women flocking to learn how to deal first-hand with all of the pesky little varmints that chew up Southern gardens with such vehemence.

The weather was perfect. The crowd was excellent, and every lady came equipped with her garden notebook so as not to miss a word. The professor, who turned out to be an entomologist, was tall and lanky and looked like everyone thought he would. He had two fascinating wisps of hair that appeared to be trained into pointed tufts, not unlike bug antennae, and the heavy black horned-rim glasses with the thick lenses helped confirm the fact that here indeed was a man who knew insects intimately. He had a nice easy accent that smacked of Boston, along with a slight little speech eccentricity—he inserted an "ug guh" between about every third phrase.

We learned, ug guh, that in spite of Raid spray bombs, we could pile all of the insects in the world over here on this side of a tremendous scale, and all the people and animals on this other side, and guess what? The insects would weigh down their side of the ug guh scale!

On the little Isle of Cyprus in one year 1,300 tons of locust eggs were destroyed, but in spite of that the locust eggs that escaped destruction totaled one hundred billion. We were told that the adaptability of insect tribes and their willingness to cooperate with their leaders are the real reasons that the little fellows are so successful and enterprising. We learned everything there was to learn about the social habits of vermin, and how lady bugs devour mealy bugs, and the motions the stag beetle makes with his jaws when he chews. We know now the simple way to differentiate between the back feet of a mole cricket and a scorpion fly, though if you do not remember the exact colors, it could be easy to become confused, more perhaps than we ug guh were at that moment.

Yes, yes, we were agreed. This was all wonderful, but after that first hour of listening and learning, the audience was getting restless. They had been waiting expectantly to hear how to get rid of thrips, aphids, rose slugs, leafhoppers, white scale and black rot so familiar to Georgia gardeners. The audience began to shift and wriggle, and one by one they folded their little notebooks and snapped shut their ball point pens. They looked out of the windows and probably began to ponder that imponderable problem that confronts universal womanhood every day and that comes into focus whenever there is time to think about it—what can we have for supper tonight?

The hostesses for this talkathon could envisage the pandemonium that was no doubt taking place that very moment at the residence of the member who was to entertain the visitors and our club members at the fanciest luncheon of the season. Everybody had been expected at 12:30 there, a good twenty minutes' drive away, and the minute hand was now heading on for one o'clock.

No one could get close enough to Gertrude to give her a quick kick, for she was safely ensconced on the podium between ex-roommate and ex-roommate's current roommate. She might well have been in Gunddagai so far as communicating with her was concerned, as she sat gazing into space either entranced or unconscious. It was impossible to catch her eye.

When another desperate quarter hour had passed, one more daring member on the front row gave a ladylike little "psst," and Gertrude returned to this world in time to see a few quick hand signals, some watch pointing, and a speech-school lip movement that looked very much like TELL-HIM-TO-SHUT-UP.

Gertrude shrugged her shoulders and turned her palms upward, but fortunately the smoke signals must have reached Big Chief Ug Guh's squaw. She leaned forward and gingerly gave his coat a yank, and it was like sorcery. He gave a few short ug guhs, a thankewsomuch, but before he sat down he mentioned something that he admitted had slipped his mind. This was to please notify those nice ladies who were planning the luncheon to not bother about him for he was not only a vegetarian but never ate in the middle of the day. "But, thanks all the same, ladies . . . there's nothing like Southern hospitality."

———

Another program chairman I well remember was a member of a Business Women's Club where I was asked to give a book review. Arriving early, I slid unnoticed into a back row chair, opened up the old knitting bag, adjusted the needlepoint, and waited for the meeting to begin. These women were smart, alert and successful, so they would know everything about businesslike procedure.

The meeting was well organized and conducted. No one spoke out of turn. The president was an intelligent, tall, well-dressed brunette with a smart little hat. An executive in her own right, she had the situation too well in hand for me to gather anything here but a few How-To notes, no How-Not-To jottings. At least that was what I thought until she called on the Program Chairman.

CHAIRMAN: If everyone will be quiet now, I want to call on our Program Chairman to tell us what she has in mind for next year before we have our year book printed. Frances, do you and your committee have our new programs lined up yet? We can't hear you back there, Frances; you'll have to come up to the front. I said, we can't hear you back there, Frances, please come to the front . . . that's right.

PROGRAM CHAIRMAN: (wending her way in and out among the folding chairs): Well, I certainly didn't know I was going to have to make a speech . . . I look a sight . . . didn't even have time to go home and get dressed . . . we're taking inventory, and I just got here. Move over, Lisa, and let me get through here. Well, (glancing at her notebook) I'm sure you all aren't going to like some of these programs, but you know you voted to have something educational this year and only use volunteer speakers . . uh, the Sulfura Club has a budget set up for this sort of thing, but we don't even give the speakers a present. Last year I don't think we even wrote them a note.

CHAIRMAN: Let's not get back on that discussion, Frances. Remember we voted on all that at the last meeting, and any-way this is a much smaller club than the Sulfura, and I don't think it's right to compare them . . . let's hear the report now . . . SSSHHH!

PROGRAM CHAIRMAN: Well, when we voted to have some-thing educational, as I said, the Committee thought it might be a good idea to find out some of the interesting things about our city, so our first program is going to be about our city hospi-tals.

MEMBER IN BACK ROW: I can't see anything educational about

hospitals. I could tell you more about hospitals than any speaker. I've had four operations in the last six years, and my mother was at University Hospital all spring. In fact, she's supposed to go back in next week for a check-up.

CHAIRMAN: Let Frances finish, Kathleen.

KATHLEEN (in whisper to Eloise next to her): We couldn't get a night nurse the first week Mama was there, and I had to sit up with her all night and then go to work the next morning. I can tell you that about killed me. I tried to take part of my vacation then, but Mr. Swanson said . . .

CHAIRMAN: SSSHHH!

ELOISE (in low whisper): That was sort of like the TV program last night. This old woman, she brought her daughter into the emergency room, and she was old and sick herself, and the poor girl, they couldn't get a nurse for her, and the pitiful old mother . . .

CHAIRMAN: SSSHHH!

PROGRAM CHAIRMAN (still talking): . . . and this doctor who's going to speak to us in October, is he upset up about Medicare! He said he was in England last summer and he made quite a study of what's been done over there too.

CHAIRMAN: What's he going to talk about—Medicare or the hospitals in Augusta, Frances? What's his topic?

PROGRAM CHAIRMAN: We haven't gotten around to that yet, but I'll get it all down before the program goes to the printers. Now, let's see . . . November . . . November oh, yes, we're going to have one of the secretaries in the Mayor's office tell us some of the things that go on in a busy day at the Mayor's office. I wrote her name down on this envelope . . . oh, well, I'll find it. And in December . . .

MEMBER (holding up her hand): Aren't we going to have the Christmas party in December?

PROGRAM CHAIRMAN: I didn't hear anything about a Christmas party, Madame Chairman, and I've already asked the Bell Ringers Choir to sing Christmas carols.

CHAIRMAN: Let's get on with the meeting tonight, ladies, and bring this up later. Is that agreeable to everybody? Will someone put that in the form of a motion? Yes, that's right—just move that we postpone the discussion of the program until next month. All right, Frances, you can sit down now. I'll check with you before you go. What's that? Frances said for somebody to look back there and see where she left her handbag. Next, we'll have the report from the Finance Committee . . .

Introductions: How Do They Do?

The introduction received by an experienced performer, or a plain everyday amateur talker, often is instrumental in launching her onto the right or the wrong foot as she steps into her act.

One of the worst offenders is the monosyllabic introducer who is either tongue-tied or insufficiently prepared to give enough data about the "introducee." This person will probably barely rise from her chair as she makes the introduction. She will no doubt keep her chin so far down and her eyes so downcast that she could be making a close examination of the design on the carpet. She will make a few low mumbling noises appreciated only by ears in the first few rows, then hastily plop back into her seat and contemplate her belt buckle thoughtfully.

The audience, instead of being attentive as the speaker rises, will collectively begin to wonder . . . Who is this character? What is her name? Where is she from? What is she going to talk about? Why is she here? What are her qualifications? Who does she think she is anyway?

I have a vivid recollection of this type of introduction. I was to give a talk to several hundred women at an Officers' Wives Club at a large army fort. The program was to be a satire, a takeoff on the flower arrangement classes this group had recently completed, using nationally-accredited flower show point scoring and rules as a guide.

The demonstration began with a Hogarth curve fashioned from a wire coat hanger, and flowers of clashing colors (fuchsia and orange) being attached with clothes pins; a hospital arrangement using a bed pan and pill bottles; a "Life Begins at Forty" niche utilizing such accessories as bifocals, Dr. Scholl's foot creams, a palmetto fan, and a bottle of Lydia E. Pinkham's elixir, and mythical "Hot Flash" roses.

The demonstrations were half over before the officers' wives felt free to take part in the fun because, having been presented by one of those soft-spoken monosyllabic sisters as "I'm sure our speaker Mizware needs no introduction," the "Mizware" had sounded not unlike the name of a visiting three star general's wife. Consequently, the officers' wives were being so careful with their military protocol that they did not know whether to smile or salute.

————

Once at a PTA meeting the speaker was presented only as "Mrs. Mmffbk who will talk about antique furniture." As this lady bore quite a resemblance to the county nurse, there was considerable confusion among the mamas as to why the R.N. who looked down the children's throats on the third Tuesdays and always recommended tonsilectomies or shots, would know anything about antique furniture.

Mrs. Mmffbk was really Mrs. Mifflebank from the Odds and Ends Antique Shop. Her husband was the manager of the new chemical plant being constructed in Augusta, and all this was featured in a big front page spread that morning in the local press.

Mrs. Mifflebank was a graduate of the National Fine Arts Institute, had owned her own decorating shop on Madison Avenue in New York, was a member of the Williamsburg Restoration Committee, and had written a book on furniture designs of the mid-Georgian period in the American Colonies. She did not go into any of these details for modesty's sake, and she was well into her talk before the audience began to discover that here indeed was a lady who knew her mahogany.

The antithesis of Mrs. Mumbles is the introducer with the long memory who shows up with the pedigree, or "Who's Who," presentation. She might even go back to the time when today's speaker, Mrs. Snortz, was little Abbie Stellmyer and at 14 was on the city all-star basketball team. She might carry Abbie right through high school and college, not only pointing out what diplomas she earned, but what Girl Scout badges she received for General Excellence. Of course, there was that big day back in 1948 when as a school girl studying Home Ec at Richmond Academy, little Abbie was awarded first prize in the homemade pickle division of the State Fair.

Mrs. Snortz, nee Abbie Stellmyer, who was only planning a brief ten-minute chat on "Planting Herbs in My Garden," was scared silly anyway, and was so busy trying to decide whether to explain that it was not herself but her older sister Sylvia who had done all those things, that she almost forgot to rise when the applause began. All she wanted to do was to read her little piece and climb into a hole before the ten-minute period allotted her was up.

That most diabolical of all introducers is the garrulous gal who tantalizes the speaker and the audience with no notes and no inhibitions. Mrs. Gaygirl leaps to her feet, tells a few hilarious jokes that have no relation to the program at hand, and then goes on to tell the audience what a treat they have in store. The speaker, Mrs. Blushing, is a SCREAM . . . she's a RIOT! Her talk is going to be SO funny that the audience will scarcely be able to stand it. In fact, she has to admit that she almost goes into hysterics just THINKING about how funny the talk will be. She is undaunted by the fact that this information is received by the audience in stony silence.

"I can't recall the exact title of her speech, but it has something to do with a take-off on modern poetry, and you can't tell the real poetry from some of the phony stuff," she shrieks, as she wipes the tears from her eyes. "I don't have my notes here, girls, because I left them in my other bag . . . my CARPET BAG!"

Mrs. Gaygirl's intimate pals by this time are doubled up with paroxysms of laughter, because this is the BIG JOKE. Mrs. Gaygirl adds a few extra "r's" now in every word, because as everybody knows, she is a transplanted Yankee, and any reference to the rolling of r's or her large tapestry handbag being called a carpet bag are always good for a few convulsions.

Mrs. Blushing, a former teacher of English at a girl's college, normally is a bit of a wag and is endowed with a sense of humor which has always been appreciated among her students, friends, and family. She would definitely be considered more of a private talker than a public speaker. At this moment nothing is very funny. The whole point of her little oration was a spoof of modern poets and modern poetry. She was going to mix in some of her own creations that made no sense at all among the more abstract ones of famous modernists. She was planning to sneak up on her audience and let these poetry lovers here to-day attempt some analyzing before she let them in on her secret. She would compare modern poetry and modern art, bringing in the famous story about the baboon in California that won the modern art prize.

But now, as she gets to her feet and faces her glum audience, she feels anything but jolly. The only thing she can concentrate on for the moment is how dearly she would like to punch Mrs. Gaygirl right in the nose and make a hasty retreat out that side door with the big red lighted letters—EXIT.

———

Sometimes the introduction of speakers is not planned on the agenda properly, a minor concern to some feminine introducers, but on occasions rather startling for the speaker. This happened to an illustrious two star general. He had already been properly introduced at a Ladies' Literary Society. As he started to rise to speak, one of the most elderly of the dowager members remembered that something had inadvertently been omitted from the routine agenda. She explained that it had been a custom of the club for over forty years for some member to give a brief biography of a famous author, and a little quotation from the Author's works.

"Of course, of course." The general stood back and waited. "Go ahead with your procedure."

The author who was discussed this day was the famous nineteenth-century writer, Mary Ann Evans, best known under her pen name of George Eliot. Then came the quotation which had been carefully memorized by an elderly little woman wearing a huge pink flowered hat.

She ended her short speech dramatically with appropriate gestures, and smiled cordially at the General as she said:

" 'Blessed is that man who having nothing to say, thereby abstains from wordy evidence of the fact.' Thank you. Now we will hear from our visiting General."

Sometimes even a thoroughly competent president has her problems if the timing of a meeting has not been checked. On one occasion every detail had been attended to in advance. A distinguished, nationally known minister was speaking to several organizations in one day and was attempting to adhere to a tight schedule.

It was a program for a church auxiliary, a *very* special program known as the Annual Meeting, and everybody was there. The President had completed the business at hand in preparation for the arrival of the speaker. The church pianist was tinkling away, and bowers of spring flowers in massive brass urns on the platform added a festive note to the long anticipated occasion.

The rustle amid the audience of ladies subsided as the speaker arrived and took his place. The music stopped, and the president stepped to the podium to welcome the guest. She had the situation well in control, with one small exception.

PRESIDENT: Good afternoon. We are delighted to have such a large gathering to hear our distinguished guest. But before I introduce him, I must take a minute to have the report from the Chairman of the Wednesday Night Supper Committee. While all of the circle chairmen are here together, the Chairman will announce the menu so that each circle will know what they are to bring. May I have that report now, please? (Silence) Does anyone know who is Supper Chairman for Wednesday Night? I don't seem to have it in my book. (Silence again. Finally . . .)

MRS. A: Well, I guess maybe I am, but I'm not sure. Margaret was supposed to be supper chairman for the month of April. She said something to me about maybe doing it if she was out of town. Does anybody know if Margaret is back yet?

MRS. B: Madame President, I'm not on the supper committee, and I don't know anything about it, but I did hear that Margaret's sister is in the hospital in Atlanta, so I doubt if she will be back by Wednesday.

PRESIDENT: Thank you, Mrs. B. Now, Mrs. A, will you please take over as Supper Chairman and plan the menu, and contact each circle chairman about what they are to bring? And now . . .

MRS. A: Well, I don't know how I am going to do that. I haven't the vaguest idea who is on that committee. Margaret asked me to help if she was not back, but she just went off and didn't call me back or anything.

MRS. B (glancing at the speaker): Madame President, I make a motion that the menu be left up to Mrs. A, and that she appoint her own supper chairman. (This motion is seconded.)

PRESIDENT: Will all those in favor say aye; those opposed, no. The motion is carried. Now . . .

MRS. C: Madame President, I'm in favor of that motion all right, but I do want to say right now that I don't think we should have ham again. We have had baked ham for the past four suppers.

PRESIDENT: Thank you for you suggestion, Mrs. C, but I think as . . .

MRS. D: And macaroni and cheese casseroles! We've had that for the past three suppers. With so many people on diets they can't eat all of those starchy casseroles. Fried chicken is something that everybody likes.

MRS. C: Well, I certainly would not call fried chicken any-

"OUR SPEAKER TODAY NEEDS NO INTRODUCTION, WHICH IS PROBABLY A GOOD THING BECAUSE FOR THE MOMENT I CAN'T THINK OF HER NAME.."

thing suitable for people on diets, even though it is fried in Ma-
zola.

MRS. B: I think we have too many desserts. Last month we
had apple pie and chocolate cake. Some of the older people
won't come if they are trying to keep up with calories.

PRESIDENT (pounding gavel): Ladies, we have voted now
to let Mrs. A and her committee decide on the menu. (Turns
and smiles at the speaker, who is too concerned with winding
his watch to respond.) So, now, we have the pleasure of having . . .

MRS. D (standing and facing the entire group): You can
get those little broilers split down the middle at the A & P for
29¢, and they are not as much trouble to cook as fried chicken.

PRESIDENT: Suppose we postpone this discussion until
after . . .

MRS. B: Tossed green salad is always good, and not as fat-
tening. Last month we had about half of that potato salad left
over. Oh, and by the way, does anyone know if I left my big
wooden salad bowl here in the church kitchen last month? It's
a large bowl . . . about this big around . . . and has sort of a
dent in one side . . . I'm sure I'd recognize it . . .

———————

Here is one introduction I well remember: "I can imagine
how disappointed you Study Club members are going to be this
morning when I tell you that after looking forward all of this
winter to hearing Dr. DeSpater review his new book, that his
plane is grounded in Atlanta. We didn't hear about it until he
called about two hours ago, so we really did get busy.

"One of our members called her friend, Mrs. Ware, who
writes the Book Review page for the paper, and she is going to
substitute for us. She is a volunteer speaker and doesn't charge

anything. That means that we can save the money we were going to pay Dr. DeSpater, and next month we can use that to have a really good program."

———————

But my very favorite of all introductions was this one: "Today, ladies, our program is to be on Robert's Rules of Order, and I'm sure our speaker needs no introduction. It's good that she doesn't because for the moment I can't think of her name."

Speaking of Speakers

If you ever find yourself seated near the speaker's table at any organizational clambake, and you observe closely the expressions on the feminine dignitaries, even an untrained eye can discover the amateur speaker in the line-up. Her face will either be ashen or flushed, according to her age. She will pick about, bird-like, at her food, adjust her hair-do continuously, drink too much coffee, and ever so often attempt a few quick squints at her notes. She might wear a very strained smile which a novice "speaker-watcher" could misconstrue as expressing poise and self-confidence.

Actually this fidgety martyr is feeling anything but poised and self-confident. As her heart pounds, her throat throbs, and her solar plexus churns, she could be saying to herself, "How did I *ever* get myself into this predicament? That scheming woman said to me, 'Darling, we just want you to give a little book review to our club!' I didn't have any idea it would be like this. Why, there must be 10,000 women in this room.

"Now I'm starting to feel funny, like something is happening to my head. Could it be softening of the brain? But I don't believe that comes on this suddenly. Maybe it's a slight heart attack . . . but I read somewhere that you first get a pain in your left arm, and mine is more in my stomach. Suppose I should start to open my mouth and no sound comes out, like in a nightmare when you try to scream for help!

"Well, I do have my notes all typed out at least, and if I don't fall over and can ever get started, I'll do all right . . . that is, if I can remember all those rules in that speaker's handbook. Maybe I can try to count the rules off on my fingers while they are reading these reports . . . let's see . . .

"Number one: Rise gracefully from your chair, keeping your feet together, and hips turned sideways to the audience to give you a trim appearance, as well as to establish your equilibrium so you won't teeter-totter.

"Number two: Stand with shoulders back, stomach in, chin up and never let the body droop.

"Number three: Smile casually, glance at your audience cordially, and then count to ten before you begin to speak. This gets you off on the popular 'slow cow' method . . . That was Greta Garbo's big secret. She was reputed to have learned to act by observing how cows chewed their cuds or strolled about the pasture with nonchalant composure . . . how now brown cow . . .

"Number four: Keep your eyes moving from one face to another as you speak, so you do not stare blankly into space.

"Number five: Grasp your notes firmly in your left hand, leaving the right hand free for natural and spontaneous gestures. Be careful not to distract your audience by using your hands unnecessarily—sliding objects back and forth, scratching, pulling on your ears, or fumbling with clothing, jewelry or face.

"Number six: As you speak, be sure to shape each word and

syllable distinctly, and curb that Southern accent, remembering not to swallow your r's and your ing's. Try to make them think you are from Schenectady or Syracuse.

"Number seven: Always be unaffected and relaxed before your audience . . . and then where did that part come in about being careful not to flap your arms? I must try to remember that . . . don't flap your arms . . . smile . . . shoulders back . . . chin up . . . watch that accent . . . be natural, poised, relaxed . . . don't flap your arms . . . oops, here I go . . ."

On the other hand there is the old virtuoso who has been around so long she has forgotten those rules if she ever knew them. She will rise to her feet and stay there enchanting her own ears with her own vocal cords. Some of these hearty souls can drone on volubly on any subject, any place, any time, often without adequate preparation or regard for the squirming audience.

Even though the speaker might know her subject, and on occasions have all of the self-confidence necessary, things can go wrong, and they often do. For instance, one day I was asked to a women's patriotic organization at a late hour. It was Flag Day and the flags failed to arrive, so as a fill-in I was asked to give the Daughters a little brush-up on conducting meetings— "just a few of the highlights on parliamentary law, my child," the president had said on the telephone.

Even though I was familiar with the organization's average membership age, that flattering category which automatically placed me a few generations down the line was the bait, and I swallowed it. My child! "Yes, I'd be glad to come," I had answered eagerly, and with renewed vigor had dashed up the stairs two at a time to decide what outfit to wear.

The event was to take place in one of the oldest and coldest homes in Augusta . . . "of much historical significance," the Home and Garden guide book had described it, "with 17 foot ceilings and spacious halls and drawing rooms filled with rare family antiques." It was a bitterly cold day for Augusta, and being familiar with heating systems in Victorian houses I knew that this was the occasion to don the new extra-heavy heliotrope suit with the hat to match.

"Madame should not wear a blouse with this exclusive little tweed number," the superior saleslady had explained. "It just isn't done with this type of suit. You see, madame, the heliotrope velvet collar and cuffs and the same trim on the hat complement each other, and a white blouse would be unthinkable! It would destroy the whole youthful effect. Just wear this little costume on occasions when the weather is sure to be cold and it is not necessary to remove your coat." The occasion was here.

Arriving as the business session of the meeting was getting under way, I was seated in the long, drafty hall that extended from one end of the large home to the other, and a cold wind kept whipping about my feet. The warm woolen suit felt snug and comfortable.

First, there was a folksy little welcome and a business meeting of sorts. Next, shooting straight from the hip, Madame President broke the bad news to them that, in spite of its being Flag Day, there would be no Flag Day program because there were no flags, or words to that effect. Any pinch hitter is always viewed with mild suspicion, be it in baseball or speechmaking, so I did not feel too warmly welcomed as I made my way between the conglomeration of everything from Victorian stools to Jacobean throne chairs carved from teakwood. I was again glad that I wore my warmest suit for the cool reception I felt coming on—the chairman had spoken those dirty words, *parliamentary law*. By this time I had become accustomed to the response to those dread words. You could almost hear what the audience was thinking . . . "Well, if I had known, I certainly wouldn't have come out on an afternoon like this to hear about Robert's Rules of Order."

I made my way to the front of the living room, a large and delightfully warm parlor, filled to capacity with a bevy of older women. Behind the small space reserved for the speaker was a large carved white marble fireplace where red embers glowed from smoldering logs. A pleasant, warm and hospitable atmosphere was prevailing after all.

As in most home meetings where there is an overflow crowd, the speaker usually knows that she will be in very close contact, so is prepared to stand and play footsie with the front row of her audience. On this day there was space only for a wobbly, undersized, three-legged table for my bag and gloves, and the foot room was not more than one square yard. I glanced back at the lazy log fire which was giving off little crackling sounds. The logs had burned down to a soft, pleasant glow, and the warmth felt good on my chilled legs and feet.

"Good afternoon, ladies," I began. "Your president has asked me to fill in today with a . . ."

"Excuse me, ma'am," a husky colored boy wearing a white coat moved in behind me. His arms were loaded with three logs so tremendous that they must have been shipped from a redwood forest in California. Nothing that large is ever cut for firewood in Georgia. He finally succeeded in getting his burden placed properly in the fireplace, and he poked and jabbed vigorously at the glowing logs with such force that they took on new life and burst into flames. Before I completed my introduction, there was a roar and a holocaust going on behind me in the fireplace. I could feel the backs of my nylon hose tightening up with the heat and could almost sniff the wool of my skirt beginning to scorch.

With a few apologetic remarks about everybody moving back a bit, I stood away from the fire as far as possible without trampling on the feet of the ladies seated in the first row. My thoughts began to be more and more confused as the blaze grew higher and brighter. I kept moving as best I could in that small area from one side of the fireplace to the other without actually hopping. I kept wondering what would happen if I gave way to impulse and squatted down and gave the calves of my legs a good scratching. There was no use asking anyone to move back again, as they were packed in already in sardine style so that everyone's knees were shoved against the chair in front.

"Main motions presented to an assembly usually introduce a new subject and are made when no other question is pending," I panted. It was good that my speech was typed and could be read, for to have spoken extemporaneously would have been fatal. I might have gone off about Yogi Bear and forest fires. Then, something queer began to happen to my new Eternally Young face powder base and Exotic Eye makeup. These had been used on such rare occasions that this was the first time they had been put to the heat and perspiration test. I fumbled toward the little table for a handkerchief in my handbag, but the table had proved too fragile. My bag and gloves had toppled to the floor and been pushed far under a chair.

I read on: "If there is a proposal to amend an amendment on the floor, the correct procedure is . . ."

I thought: I hate to mop my face with the velvet cuff of this new suit, but I have to do something. I can feel this powder base running down my chin. To make matters worse, my glasses are clouding up. Wonder if I can read without them. Yes, if I squint and move the book out at arm's length, I can read quite clearly.

Once, in a fever of forgetfulness, I unbuttoned the two top buttons of my coat. Fortunately I recalled in time that the cool white nylon blouse was in a plastic bag tucked away in a drawer at home, so the buttons were quickly shoved back in place.

"We're not in any hurry, my child," the president had told me on the telephone, "and after your talk maybe the ladies would like to ask questions and we could have a little question-and-answer period." I glanced at my watch; I had only been cooking for a quarter of an hour but I was surely done. Strangely enough, the ladies did not seem bored at all, and I began to wonder if they were sincerely engrossed in learning parliamentary procedure or if they had a morbid curiosity to see which portion of my anatomy was barbecued first.

The last part of the outline went by as fast as I could turn the pages and runthewordstogether, for I could see what was happening in the dining room. The boy in the white coat was making his way slowly but surely through the chairs carrying two more of those giant logs for the burnt offering!

―――――――

In the category of speakers there are all kinds. Some of the worst are the cultured cultural speakers. "Real appreciation of modern poetry is a state of existicism in cultural acceleration," explained Mrs. Lessinger B. Sorrell IV to the Friday Morning Study Club. Mrs. Sorrell was known as a "published poet" so any opinions she might toss out were treated with respect.

"Truly inspired poets express their innermost thoughts on wings of fantasy," she continued, "and we can compare their flights of ideas as gossamer wings. We must capture them quickly, for in a fleeting moment the little germ of an idea is born, lives and breathes, then dies and is lost forever. Even the very poets who give birth to these ideas cannot explain the exact meaning at a later time. Poetry is such a delicate thing that we must not be too critical, for often the true meaning is lost in the analytical mind of one who is not highly imaginative . . ."

Several ladies wrinkled their brows and glanced around to see if anyone else was puzzled. Perhaps as the speaker delved further into the subject it might become a trifle clearer. The members listened attentively as she continued.

"The soul must be liberated in verse, and immersed in soft pools of dreams and ideas, with no restraint on the subconscious. As Shelley has told us, 'The fountains mingle with the river, and the rivers with the ocean.' Little thoughts mingle with big thoughts and little dreams with big dreams, and there is unity, unity, unity!"

Some of the older members leaned forward in their chairs on the last "unity," and two front row occupants adjusted their hearing aids. Mrs. Sorrell folded her hands on her ample chest and looked skyward. "Provocative poetry is not something that can be analyzed like a mathematical problem," she explained, "but brings into focus a wonderment of the mysterious portent or fortune of life, and this sometimes fades into oblivion with the humdrum of daily living. Oh, that we all could capture these priceless pronouncements of variable moods, as they float in and out of our consciousness and into the essence of fulfillment! Do I make myself clear?"

The Friday Study Club assented in unison and continued to pay even closer attention.

"Let me give you a lucid example," Mrs. Sorrell went on, as she scrambled and scratched about in a frayed brown notebook that spewed out endless loose sheets of paper which scattered over the speaker's table. She pounced on one yellowish, dog-eared sheet that looked as if it had been rescued from some archive, and continued.

"Here is one of my own poems that I would like to read to you if I may, for it does express so well what I am telling you. I shall never forget when I wrote this. My late husband, the doctor, and I were visiting the mountains that summer . . . that was quite a while before he passed, you know . . . and it was sunset. I stole away from our friends to a secluded spot, for I could definitely feel a poem coming into focus.

"Now, I must explain that the doctor, before he passed, was not too understanding about these things, and many of you ladies have no doubt suffered the same humiliation from your dear husbands who . . . well, are not too sympathetic with poetry, and, if you've had that experience, you know what I mean. Anyway, that afternoon I left my group of friends and climbed alone to a little summer house atop Mt. Kosku, and I hope all of you lovers of poetry can go back to that spot with me now as I read to you these thoughts that I captured for posterity. I have called it *Whether or Whether Not*—

Sunset on the mountain; Oh, come let us rise to the music Oh
    rhythms and beats. Harken, dear one,
As the wings of evening descend, and there are the calls of the
    wood creatures
Which may or may not be uttered or understood.
But who am I to say what aught I know with earthly ears

And sweep to the fields and plains below
Without question, my soul tells me again and again.

What ho, gentle wind and the little flowers
Of non-existent lights that may or may not flicker,
And might come once again as dawn does first and then night.
Under leaves that are tumbled and ruffled like feathers,
Where once a song bird lived, but who was toppled into his
      bier
By mortal man, the proud hunter with his gun so bold.
Whither is the multitude that passed this way
And mere man cradled in his weary heart these secrets,
Or whether or whether not.

There was a faint patter of white gloves, cleared throats, and
chairs being pushed back. Our modern muse was still standing with palms pressed prayerfully together and eyes closed,
and the spell which had been cast still hovered about. It will
never be known "Whether or Whether Not" the Friday Study
Club learned about modern poetry, for they were spared the
necessity of revealing their innermost thoughts by a sudden
change of mood. Lights were suddenly switched on. Someone
rapped on a glass for attention and announced in a loud, clear
voice: "Will whoever has a blue Buick, license number 6-2630,
please come to the side entrance. You're blocking the driveway,
and it's starting to rain. Blue Buick number 6-2630, please move
your car . . ."

———————

One of the most popular of all programs for smaller groups
is a club's own beloved member with her LET-ME-TELL-
YOU-ABOUT-MY-TRIP color slides. Rarely indeed do we
find a selfish traveler, one who refuses to share happy reminis-

cences, either orally or "slide-ly," with everyone, friend or foe.

At one meeting I attended, the program chairman, the club president, the hostess and the happy traveler busied themselves getting the dining and breakfast room chairs and garden furniture dragged into the living room so that everybody could see "Maggie's wonderful slides." Other helpful members crawled under tables in the manner of unladylike she-crabs searching for an electrical outlet that was electrified.

Finally, the electric shocks found their way across several loosely-joined, ratty-looking extension cords which kept separating as chairs and feet shifted. At last the show was on the road and ready to go. Lights out . . . but there was a slight delay. The projector resting on the low coffee table shone its light at least fifteen inches below the tipsy shimmering silver screen, which had been erected by a couple of feminine unmechanical engineers who had been introduced for the first time to a folding tripod.

The lights flashed back on again, and as the coffee table was piled higher and higher with sturdy reference books, the projector light finally made contact with the screen. Lights off again . . . the moment had arrived. The program chairman rose boldly in the darkness and began to speak. "Maggie, we are glad to have the opportunity to see the slides that you and John took of gardens on your European trip. You are generous to share them with us for our program today, and everyone is looking forward to learning about European gardens." (clap, clap).

Out of the gloom and from under the coffee table came Maggie's voice, a faint thank-you. She pulled herself up from her knees and puffed: "This first slide is the one John took of the boat we went on, only you're supposed to call it a ship when it's big. See, there are the letters, the *S.S. Constitution*. You can't read it . . . wait a minute . . . I have this one upside down. Will somebody please turn on the overhead light. I can't see with this flashlight very well . . . now, here it is, it's in straight now. It was raining the day we sailed and you can't see it too clearly, but that white part you see, that's the side of the boat.

"Whoops, there's something wrong with this projector so don't bother to catch the slides. They always shoot out that way and pop across the room. We pick them up afterwards. It's less confusing."

The audience was obviously fascinated by this rare mechanical device, for each time the machine clicked another slide soared across the room, zigzagging at astounding speed. Heads bobbed back and forth, and people began to raise hands and arms in front of their faces as protection against these tiny flying objects.

"Here we are going out of New York harbor," Maggie continued. "If you look closely I think you can see the Statue of Liberty, or it might be the Empire State Building. Here we are on deck . . . just a second . . . I don't know how that got in there. Anyway, those people in those Dutch costumes live on Marken Island, near Amsterdam. The people dress like that, too, wooden shoes and all.

"Don't keep walking in front of the projector, Flo, go back of the chair—whoops, there went two slides under the sofa—don't try to pick them up, girls.

"Now, let's see. Oh, this is the one I was looking for. Here we are back on the *Constitution*. That couple with us are from St. Louis and he kept singing 'Meet me in St. Louis, Louie' . . . he was hilarious. He won the Funny Hat Contest with a plastic picked chicken tied on his head. Watch that slide, Flo. It's on the window sill.

"Now here . . . this is when we are getting into Gibraltar. It was cloudy that day and we didn't get a good picture, but it was interesting to see that big rock. It didn't look like it does in the Prudential Insurance ads, but you approach it from another side. It is a little blurred but you can see the outline. Don't step on that slide. They're all over the floor but I'll get them later.

"Wait a minute, this slide won't get in right. Here it goes. That must be in the wrong place because that looks like the hotel in Frankfurt . . . or it could be that restaurant we liked in Lucerne. I'm not sure. John didn't go through these slides very well. I thought those pictures of the gardens and flowers around Cannes and Nice were in this first box. They are the ones I wanted you to see. Turn the light on, Ann, and let me look through here. The flowers were in full bloom, and I kept telling John, 'the girls in the garden club would have a fit if they could see these flowers over here.' Turn the lights off, Ann. Here, this was taken in Vence, that's near Cannes and the place where they make the perfume. It's a little gray, but that was the color of the building. Watch those slides under the table.

"This was taken from the car going up the mountain, and in the background you can see the flowers that they use to make the perfume. What happened? Someone has pulled the extension cord . . . we can't find it over here. Pull up the shades, Genie, so we can see where these cords have separated . . . No, that's all right with me. Flo says she's going on and serve the coffee and sandwiches because it's almost 12 o'clock and some of them have to go early. Pick up the slides everybody and I'll be looking through this other box. I know they're in here. John went through every one of these last night . . . at least he said he did, and he said he had fixed that little dohickey that throws the slides but he didn't. No cream, thank you, I'll just have mine black."

————

In Atlanta, the year book of a garden club had listed for the March meeting a talk to young mothers, the subject being "Early Habits in Infant Training," by Dr. H—— H——. The good doctor was unable to fulfill his commitment, so the chairman went to the front, opened up a little book, and explained to the members: "Ladies, I have an announcement to make today. In our year books you will see that today we were planning to have a special program for the young mothers in the club, entitled "Early Habits in Infant Training," but as Dr. H—— H—— was unable to be with us, we have been most fortunate in getting a substitute. One of our own garden club members is going to fill in with a most informative talk entitled, 'Potting Can Be Fun'."

————

When a woman has a special hobby and pursues it unwaveringly for years, often to her it is of such importance that it more or less blots out whatever else is taking place in the world. If you have known many ardent horticulturists, you will understand.

In a nearby college town at the Faculty Wives Study Club, the speaker was an expert on the planting and growing of bulbs. As a willing volunteer, this bulb devotee had been generous with her time as a speaker, her gifts of bulbs to the members or organizations of the University, and with assistance in landscaping problems.

Finally, one of the lady professors, while expressing the gratitude of the faculty members, inquired if the kind lady would be willing to accept an honorarium from the University in appreciation of her unselfish and helpful services.

The recipient of this praise was modest as well as unselfish, for she was quick to reply: "I do appreciate that, but you know, I love sharing what I have learned about gardening with everybody. And, frankly, I don't think these little talks I've been giving on bulbs are important enough for the University to give me an honorary degree—but honey you tell them that I appreciate it all the same."

———————

Speaking of speakers, sometimes it is not the speaker who wilts before an audience, but the panic-stricken introducer, like the little woman who gulped: "I'd like to say something nice about our speaker today, but I can't think of anything to say."

Conventions: Women Versus Women

Would you like to listen in on a delegate being instructed how to vote at a national Garden Club convention? At a special called meeting following the general session, Bertha, a club member with a taste for detail in fashion, was making this suggestion even before the president had called the meeting to order.

"I feel that if Emma is going as our only delegate to the convention that she should not be wearing a wool hat in April."

"Wouldn't that be up to Emma to decide? After all, this is only a committee meeting to discuss the convention with our delegate. But, Emma, I'm sure you wouldn't mind a few suggestions, would you, darling?"

Emma replied thoughtfully: "But this is a Peck and Peck suit. I ordered it out of the *New York Times* and the hat came with it. It matches, you know. They advertised it as a light-weight spring suit."

"We realize that, my dear," the president continued, "but Bertha does have good ideas about style and she feels that a straw hat the same color would look better."

Bertha lit a cigarette, crossed her legs, and sat back in the large chair in contemplation. "The convention is in April, honey, and I can tell you that it will be regular summer weather, and people *just don't wear wool hats in April*."

The President interrupted with a polite mention of getting on with the talk to the delegate, and "we want to go over these bills they are trying to present to Congress and find out what the ladies intended to do about this highway thing.

"Look, it's all here in this little leaflet from National Headquarters," she continued, "so everybody turn to the second page, paragraph 3, and it says: How to write a letter to your Congressman. Everyone should read this carefully, because not only do we want Emma to know how to vote, but we might want to complain about something sometime, and it's good to know these things."

Bertha put out her cigarette. "Emma," she said, "I think you made a mistake not to buy that pink silk suit with the jacket. It was reduced to almost half price, and when you take the jacket off it is dressy enough for a cocktail dress. And another thing, if you are going to be on the program, I don't think you should be wearing a wool hat in April."

The president continued undaunted. "Here it is. It says, 'This bill concerning the beautification of our new interstate highways is of utmost importance to every citizen. Paragraph 4, Section 3. How to write a letter to your State Senator'." She read on uninterrupted for several minutes.

Emma, the delegate, in deep reflective mood was the first to speak: "Why don't I wear the blue dress I bought for Lisa's wedding? You know, the one with the white beads."

"Wear what you want to, my dear," Bertha answered, "but when you get to that convention you'll see what I'm talking

"WHEN YOU GIRLS GET
TO THE CONVENTION BE SURE TO
FIND OUT EXACTLY HOW TO WRITE
A LETTER TO YOUR CONGRESSMAN,
IN CASE WE DECIDE TO COMPLAIN
ABOUT SOMETHING.."

about. I went last year, and I never saw so many dressed up women in my life. If I were you, I wouldn't even take that wool hat. You can borrow my new yellow one if you don't have one. They even wear flowered hats to the President's Breakfast at 7:30 in the morning!"

The secretary interrupted apologetically, "Excuse me, Madame President, but I have to pick up my car pool in five minutes, and I want to get this in the minutes. What do you think I should say about this meeting?"

The President was serious and pensive before she gave her reply. "Oh, I don't know. You might say that we had a special called meeting to instruct our delegate who is going to the National Convention. No use going into a lot of details."

Emma, the club's lone delegate, was still not to go unencumbered to the convention. For another member, whom we shall know only as "Sis," was busily pawing through her handbag, and from the chaos she brought forth a neatly folded checkbook. "Emma, let me give you this blank check before you leave and you can fill it out when you get there." Sis was talking and writing simultaneously.

"What check?"

"Don't you remember, Emma, I talked to you about the cute little antique shop near the hotel."

"I know that, but what's the check for? I don't get it."

"Wait a minute, and I'll explain it to you." Sis folded the checkbook and dropped it back amidst the clutter. "I want you to do something for me. It's no trouble at all. I want you to run by that antique shop. You go out of the hotel lobby through the entrance to the right of the desk. When you get to the street, turn left, cross that first little street, and go about half a block.

You can't miss it. There are two wrought iron benches in front and an old spinning wheel over the door.

"Now, honey," she went on, "be sure and get that man in there to wait on you. Don't mess with his wife. She's a regular old witch. She won't come down a penny on anything. I want you to see if they still have that pair of epergnes that I looked at: silver bases with cut crystal bowls on top. You can tell them because they have little do-lollies that dip in and out like this. If they are still there, try and get that man to mark them down. Don't let his wife see what you are talking about, because I know she's not going to want to reduce anything while there are over five hundred women at that convention only a block away. Just saunter in there casually and look around, and then when the convention is about over, make him an offer.

"Here is his card. See, S. Herzetog, 511 North Street, and see here's where he wrote it down . . . pair of silver and crystal epergnes, $175. See if you can't get him down to about $125 or $115. Those epergnes are exactly what I need on my sideboard."

Emma slipped the card into her wallet carefully and turned once again to go. "I'll see what I can do, Sis, but what about shipping them home? Aren't they liable to get broken?"

"*Shipping* them home!" Sis looked surprised. "Oh, that won't be necessary. Mr. Herzetog says that he can pack them into two separate boxes, and you can bring them with you on the plane. They're not but about 16 inches high. You can keep them under the seat on the plane. Mr. Herzetog does that all the time, and that way, he says, you can be certain that they won't get broken."

Emma looked subdued. Apparently dispelling any idea she might have had about enjoying the convention untrammeled by sound advice and responsibilities, she mumbled something that sounded like "Take my child to music" and made a quick departure.

———————

As for the convention, if you have ever been present at one of those simultaneous surgings of several hundred women into a hotel lobby or convention hall, then you already know what takes place. There is much conversation plus much clutching of mink stoles, unwieldy handbags, official papers, make-up cases and corsages . . . and then, more conversation.

Arriving early at one of these conventions, I found it a fascinating pastime to observe the arrival of some 583 lady delegates, 3 brave gentlemen speakers, plus 2 disconsolate looking husbands. It was even more interesting to chat with the bell captain as the big registration onslaught was coming to a close.

"Yes, ma'am," he answered as he removed his cap and wiped away the sweat from his brow. "I've been at this hotel 10 years, and we have one convention right after another, but thank goodness, most of 'em are men."

"Is there much of a difference?" I queried, knowing his probable answer. Having had this experience previously, and having also attended men's conclaves as a tag-along wife, I knew that the contrast is noteworthy.

"Let's put it this way," the bell captain explained. "All of the ladies bring about three or four pieces of luggage each, plus the things they tote. Now the men folks, they bring one bag or sometimes two. Then the ladies who come in their cars, I believe they bring all the clothes they own.

"See that line of cars out here in front of the hotel?" he pointed to the driveway. "We've only got six boys on duty this afternoon, and there must be forty cars still lined up there to park. The garage is behind the hotel. It ain't a hundred yards

. . . but none of 'em want to park their own automobiles. I tell you it's a mess 'cause they all get here about the same time, and everybody is in a big hurry."

"What about the day they all leave at the same time?" I asked him.

"Well, if anything, I believe that's worse. Last time we had one of these lady conventions, one of them, she lost her parking ticket," the bell captain recalled with little humor. "She kept saying she had a green Buick, and we looked through about 300 cars and still couldn't find it. She got so upset she had the police down here. All this was going on right after the big farewell luncheon was over and all the ladies were checking out at the same time. Finally, after nearly everybody was gone, the police said they couldn't do a thing unless they had the license number. Finally she called up her husband in Columbus. And guess what! That lady didn't have a green Buick. She had driven her husband's car and forgot about it being a Pontiac! You never heard such a fuss as she raised. And Johnny, he's a boy over there at the garage . . . she didn't give him but a dime and he'd been looking for that car nearly two hours. Some of the boys at the garage said they might not show up for work the day this thing gets over . . . they know what they're in for."

The desk clerk was the next staff member with whom I talked. It was rather a tense moment when I confronted the young man. He was busily conferring with the registration chairman, an attractive dimpled blonde with a youthful figure who could have been anywhere from thirty-five to sixty. She was meticulously coiffured and manicured and attired in a smart navy blue knit, with everything new and everything matching.

Obviously the clerk did not take a very indulgent view of the way the delegates were being registered and assigned to their rooms. Instead of the routine manner of using their names, the local committee, with the organizational complexity of women, had devised a more unique plan. The delegates were being registered according to the name of their individual garden clubs.

Unsteady card tables were placed in hazardous positions in the main lobby. Each table had been marked with a home-made sign designating letters of the alphabet, but as the crowd swarmed and pushed against the tables, those that were still pinned precariously to the card table covers could not be detected above the table level. This afforded much opportunity for gay banterings: "I'm in the Lilac Club. Where are the L's? Let's go to L, Rose." "No, you go to L, I'm going to C . . . I'm Camellia Garden Club," and on and on. It turned out to be a real frolic.

Members of the Appleseed Garden Club of Augusta pushed and shoved their way to Table ABCD. They were graciously greeted by one of the charming local hostesses and sent on their happy way to Room 506. The only hindrance was that the Appleseed Club of Augusta envelope had been plucked from the file by the Appleseed Garden Club of Athens several hours prior to this. Room 506, it turned out, was completely occupied by the two Athenian garden clubbers. They not only had well settled in, and filled every nook and cranny in the room and closets with clothing and cosmetics, but had departed for a shopping tour of the city.

The youthful clerk by this time had passed the stage of being rational, and it was difficult to explain exactly what had happened and to ask for any advice about securing other rooms. "There must be twenty clubs in Georgia called Hill Crest," he moaned. "And Hill Top and Hill Side and Hill High and Hill View." He leafed through the files, as more and more disgruntled delegates surrounded him.

That vision in navy blue, the registration chairman, knew *everybody,* and she was perfectly charming. She was constantly being interrupted and greeted with shrieks of recognition at Convention Present by old buddies of Conventions Past. She had been through this before, and if she was concerned, she kept the fact carefully concealed. "Don't worry about it, Mr. Radford," she said with a motherly pat on the room clerk's back, "everything is going to work out just fine. Everybody will get a room eventually."

"But look at this long list of ladies who have the wrong rooms," young Mr. Radford said with great apprehension. "They're not only unhappy, but some of them are getting downright belligerent."

"Let's worry about that after we serve tea," the chairman answered. "Now, we're all going into the Crystal Room for a nice cup of tea and a welcome from our National President. You and that nice Mr. . . . you know . . . Mr. What's-his-name. You all figure something out. We'll be in there about an hour. Won't that give you enough time?"

"It's them birds that have caused all the trouble this time," the headwaiter explained. "I have been here a long time, and I know how to handle these decorations and the ladies with their flowers, but this is the first time we've run into anything like this."

"Like what?" I asked, and moved into the large dining room where the banquet would be served that night. "These ladies have been bringing bird cages and birds in here all day," he replied. "They're using these little plastic cages with the fake birds along with the flowers on the tables. But all those back there in those big cages hanging on the background there . . . them's real birds."

"That's part of the theme of the convention," I explained, showing him the program. "See, it's all about Conservation."

"I don't know nothing about that, but I do know about Elmo," he said.

"Who's Elmo?"

"He's a parakeet and he lives here at the hotel. Belongs to one of our permanents, an old lady named Mrs. Lehmann."

"What happened to Elmo?" I inquired.

"Well, the ladies told me they needed one more bird cage and one more parakeet to hang up here in this tree behind the speakers' table. So I told them about Elmo, and they asked me to go talk to old Mrs. Lehmann about using Elmo as part of the decorations for tonight. Mrs. Lehmann seemed to be real pleased that Elmo was being invited to have such an important part in all the doings. She's sorta old, you know, and she don't go out much, but she takes lots of interest in everything that goes on here at the hotel. Well, I went up to her room and got Elmo and while we were hanging his cage up here on this middle limb . . . I don't see how it happened . . . but somehow the cage fell over on the side, and that derned bird took off. That's all we've been doing most of the afternoon, trying to catch Elmo. I knew Mrs. Lehmann would go all to pieces if she knew about it. She talks to that parakeet like he was a baby.

"The only thing we could do was to lock all the doors into the main dining room, and I thought we would never get those tables set up for nearly 600 people. We had to keep a boy standing at each door and let the waiters and the ladies who were decorating in and out. It was a mess, I tell you!"

The suspense was awful. I *had* to know what happened to

Elmo. "Did you ever manage to get Elmo back into his cage?"
I asked.

"We didn't get him in the cage until about half an hour ago,
and that banquet's to start in a little while. We finally had to get
the Fire Department to catch him. One of the firemen was up
here this afternoon checking about the exits and the candles,
and he went back and got a truck with a ladder that would
reach up to the ceiling. Elmo kept flying from one side of that
ridge there on this high ceiling and back to the chandelier.

"I tell you, lady, these women's conventions are bad enough
without fooling with birds. All I hope is that old Mrs. Lehmann
don't hear about it!"

———————

Later that evening the two delegates proudly representing
the Appleseed Garden Club of Augusta, Ga., were finally assigned to a room. This had been reserved in the name of the
Appleseed Garden Club of Albany, Ga., who had by mistake
moved into the quarters of the Apple Orchard Club of Macon.
Other than numerous telephone calls at all hours for the Albany delegates, everything was finally in order.

When the housekeeper came to give the room a final check,
I queried her about feminine delegates to conventions. She
shifted an armload of towels from one arm to the other, and
paused in the doorway.

"Women's conventions," she mused. "They usually mean
trouble for us, or maybe you'd call it confusion. The ladies are
nice, all right—real friendly and chatty and all that—but they
bring so much of everything that it is hard for the maids to
get into the rooms to tidy up.

"I suppose the most troublesome thing is that they lose things.
Mostly they misplace them. Especially some of the older ones

who leave their coats and sweaters all over the hotel when the air-conditioning is going. Not long ago a woman lost her mink stole. She said someone had taken it out of her closet. We had to get the house detective up here, and come to find out she had left it in her friend's room next door the night before.

"When they have these big banquets and put on those fancy evening clothes that they don't wear very often, they have zipper trouble. Sometimes it takes two people to get 'em zipped up. I've helped zip up some whose backs and shoulders popped out like canned biscuits when you open the can. I don't see how they breathe."

The housekeeper smiled as she recalled a recent experience. "The house physician had to cut one plump lady out of her zipper last month. Her friend, who admitted she couldn't see with her glasses off, had zipped up the evening dress here on the side right under the arm, and it caught in her skin. I never saw anything like that. That doctor had to take a couple of stitches after he got the zipper cut out. That lady went on to the banquet, though. She wore a beaded sweater over the bandages and took two aspirin—said she wasn't going to let a little thing like two stitches ruin her evening."

A Quizzical Quiz

When Henry Clay made the statement that he would "rather be right than president," he apparently did not know about women's club meetings. I know some charming presidents who do not give one small tittle about such tedious subjects as being right. Such a term as "protocol" to them could well be one of those new health tonics spelled backwards. Even when they are being instructed along the grim lines of parliamentary procedure, many of them have little disciplinary interest in any accepted code. In teaching this important, but often dull subject to women's groups, it is sometimes astounding to see what emerges from the brains under some of those high-styled coiffures.

In deference, however, to the great majority of club women who *do* care, and to those in my classes who have always answered quiz questions with unimpeachable accuracy, I am the first to admit that the answers unfolded herewith come from a minute minority. As the quiz sheets do not require signatures, the ladies who penned these answers shall forever remain anonymous.

QUESTION: What is an agenda?

ANSWER: A gender is the difference between men and women, for example, men are masculine gender and women are feminine gender.

QUESTION: What is a constitution?

ANSWER: A constitution is something you use in the government or in a club to tell everybody what to do. If you don't like it, you AMEN it.

QUESTION: What is a standing committee?

ANSWER: A standing committee is a committee that stands up to give their report. This way they can be heard and seen better than sitting down.

QUESTION: What are motions?

ANSWER: Motions are movements the officers and members go through, like having a show of hands, putting things on the table, writing the minutes, or having a rising vote.

QUESTION: Explain a point of order.

ANSWER: In meetings, order must be maintained to a fine point. In this way everything is orderly to a point of order.

QUESTION: What do you consider the most interesting thing you have learned in these classes on parliamentary law?

ANSWER: As we do not have to sign our names on these quizzes, I prefer to be perfectly honest. Nothing.

QUESTION: Is there a difference in postponing a motion and laying it on the table?

ANSWER: Yes, if there is no table to lay it on. In that case the thing to do is to postpone it and not mention it until the next meeting.

QUESTION: In parliamentary law what do we mean by "to commit"?

ANSWER: The same as to commit a sin, commit a crime, commit a murder, etc. If you commit something, then you've done it.

QUESTION: How do you amend a motion?

ANSWER: I really wouldn't know.

QUESTION: Can you suggest a better word than "contrary" when members are opposed to a motion?

ANSWER: In our club "contrary" is the best possible word to describe most of our members.

QUESTION: What do you think is the best method of voting in a meeting?

ANSWER: Voting with your eyes and nose.

QUESTION: If there is a request for information is there a necessity for a second?

ANSWER: When everybody is talking at once sometimes it is necessary for not only a second, but a third.

QUESTION: What does it mean when you are asked to address the chair?

ANSWER: Talk to the chair where the chairman will sit. We did that in our class today.

QUESTION: What are the duties of the treasurer?

ANSWER: The treasurer takes in all the money in the club and then spends it.

QUESTION: In parliamentary law what is meant by attest?

ANSWER: A quiz, like this thing we're having today.

QUESTION: What is a quorum?

ANSWER: A place where ancient Romans used to have meetings.

QUESTION: What is a resolution?

ANSWER: A decision to do something better, often made on New Year's Day but not necessarily.

QUESTION: What is unfinished business?

ANSWER: When everybody wants to go and the meeting keeps going on and on.

(Let us not have that happen here—shall we make a motion that this quiz be adjourned?)

Let's Meet Mr. Robert, Ladies

Brigadier General Henry Martyn Robert (West Point, 1857), author of Robert's Rules of Order, has been called the "Club Woman's Best Friend," but the epithet is debatable. Though many successful women's organizations do stand in awe of the fundamentals of that best known rule book of Parliamentary Procedure, others hit a few of the high spots here and there, but take little notice of its importance.

When a club starts to fall apart at the seams, and the membership dribbles away because of lack of interest, the cause is often because the leaders and the members lack a common denominator of proper rules. Mr. Robert may be dull, but he is steady and reliable, and he is definitely worth knowing.

Poor man, he had a miserable time being recognized almost a century ago. It took this dedicated gentleman 13 years of arduous note-gathering and writing to complete his 40,000-word rule book, and then no one would publish it. Undaunted, he had 4,000 copies privately printed, and distributed these free copies to government leaders, business men, and educators. Then, the nervous author awaited the response. It was tremendous. A young country undergoing organizational pains needed such a volume, and since then (1876) over 2 million copies have been sold.

Robert's Rules has never been surpassed for conducting meetings, even though the book is often the butt of jokes and cartoons, and even poems such as these:

The Chairman's Lament

Robert's Rule of Order,
That book is such a bore,
I wish I could ignore it,
And refer to it no more.
We always have to run our club
By "what Mr. Robert'd say,"
I only wish that he'd preside
Instead of me today.

Mr. Robert Vs. Mr. Goren

Gals who belong to women's clubs
To me are always boring.
They talk to you of Robert's Rules
Instead of Mr. Goren.
They chat about such dribble
As how a motion's made,
Instead of such important things
As how to bid a spade.
Fancy all that interest
In amending some old motion,
Instead of trying to bid a slam
If you should take a notion.

Anti-climax

At last the meeting nears its end,
Homeward the members their ways will wend,
But then at the moment of abatement,

Some dame will rise and make a statement.
From Robert's Rules why don't they learn,
Just what is meant by "LET'S ADJOURN."

Almost a century has passed since Mr. Robert began whipping up his rules which were based on those of the British Parliament. Certainly it never occurred to him that some day they would have to be interpreted by women! But, of course, neither he, nor anyone else, fancied a hundred years ago that American men would be accused of living in what is sometimes called a matriarchal society!

During General Robert's era middle-aged women were called "sweet little old ladies," and few of them entered business, attended meetings, or had activities outside of the home. They sat on the front porch wearing dainty lace caps and sensible shoes, and they crocheted and gossiped. Their outlet into the world of organization was the Missionary Society. "Gavel" to them was just so much ground-up rock to put on the driveways for the carriages.

Today, little old ladies are called Girls. If they have a front porch, it has been glassed in and is status-ly referred to as the Family Room. Anyway, the little woman is not at home to sit on the front porch. She's the one in the bright green miniskirt who has just teed off with her foursome to play nine holes before lunch.

Later, she might dash by the house to check on the family and to get the dinner out to defrost. She will make a quick change into her chic copy of a Chanel suit, her replica of a Lilly Daché hat, and her tightest foundation garment. After a few applications of some magic formula that covers up wrinkles as Kemtone conceals cracks in old wallpaper, some devastating eye shadow and the latest shade of "Luscious Lips," she will scurry off to the Women's Club looking not too many years older than her daughter.

Many of these enterprising, enthusiastic and energetic women render a unique service to their community and church which is of inestimable value and importance. They possess the uncanny ability to guide a meeting through its routine with an efficiency that would set an example for Congress.

On the other hand, the talents of many equally capable and competent women are lost forever to worthwhile service and to their own self-satisfaction and spiritual and mental growth because, as they will explain: "I don't know one thing about how a meeting should be conducted. I couldn't be chairman of anything, not even a committee. I'd be scared silly . . . honey, ask someone else. That's one thing I wouldn't even attempt . . . not me!"

One woman of great charm, beauty and intelligence whom I knew was so overcome at being chosen an officer in her club that she was unable even to rise from her seat and decline the honor. She wrote this letter instead:

Dear Fellow-members:

I know that I should consider it an honor to be elected vice-president of the Artichoke Garden Club, and I do, but I am afraid it will be impossible for me to accept. I have not slept all night. I realize that I should have said something yesterday at the meeting when my name was put up for election, and I was unanimously voted on from the floor, or whatever it is you say, but I was too terrified.

I must admit that I have never held an office in anything, and the thought of getting up before fifty women and saying anything is more than I could take on. I'm sure I would faint.

This may come as a surprise to some of you, but in spite of my being teased about talking so much, I am the most timid soul you can imagine, so please accept my resignation instead of my acceptance if that can be done according to correct parliamentary procedure. If you do this, I will promise to work on any committee where I am needed, and will also be glad to relinquish my prize as the Club Frug Champion which I won at the Club Christmas party last year.

Respectfully submitted

Laura

Another woman has said, "All women's clubs are big bores. I've heard so much about them that I don't want to join anything where I have to work." She is certain that she is avoiding being bored at a club meeting by playing bridge every afternoon or watching TV, contributing nothing to her country, community or church and growing old very ungracefully.

In days gone by woman's chief role was homemaking and motherhood, and she generally kept her own domestic production line going full steam for 14 to 16 hours a day. She had her garden, and she canned vegetables and put up her own jam without the benefit of Certo. She drew water by hand from the pump and boiled the clothes with homemade soap instead of Blue Cheer. She started from scratch when she prepared the family meals, besides pumping a foot pedal sewing machine at night by lamp light to make her family's wardrobe. By the time she banked the fire in the fireplace and crawled under the goosefeather quilt she had quilted herself, she was too pooped to dwell on whether or not she had been creative that day or had expressed herself.

Now they tell us that things like instant mashed potatoes or frozen chicken pies make housework so easy for women that they can do something drastic to their egos. The woman begins to get a fixation as to whether she is really needed by her family. It seems that she has been deprived of her natural feminine creative instincts when she misses the opportunity to hand-peel a big pan of dirty spuds or scoop out a chicken's insides.

This is someone else's idea, not mine. I've loved having my creativity curbed ever since as a bride in Melbourne, Australia, I purchased some chicken gizzards at the poultry market, fried them in deep, sizzling fat, and learned the hard way that they had not been cleaned. Our tiny kitchenette had been freshly painted, and on the day we moved from that apartment a year later we were still finding exploded kernels of corn and little pebbles that chickens eat embedded on the walls and ceiling.

One point upon which psychiatrists, psychologists, ministers, doctors, and others who are called upon for counselling are agreed is this. Women "joiners" are more normal and are happier than the hermit type female who has few interests outside of her business or home or her own family circle. Worthwhile, unselfish service for others, and taking part with other women in organized activities is group therapy for a woman, just as a night out with the boys at the Moose's Lodge is for a man.

James Thurber has put it this way. He said women should join clubs to avoid getting a "schmal haus" (small house) complex, a type of claustrophobia from being shut up in a house or an office following the same routine day after day. A club, like a hobby, is a means of finding new friends, new interests, and gateways to self-expression.

Having a job in an organization is of more importance to the individual woman than being only a member at large. This is especially true if one is inclined to be shy and retiring. (Remember that, you bold, overbearing husbands!)

Acquiring a smattering of correct rules, poise and experience in public speaking, and being an important part of something is stimulating and fun. Fun with parliamentary procedure?

Impossible! It is doubtful that our nice Mr. Robert ever had a good guffaw during all of those grim years that he was grinding out those dull, but necessary rules.

Were this gentleman alive today, I feel that once he recovered from the shock of witnessing some routine ladies' meeting where his precious rules were being applied, that he might have been vastly amused. After sitting in on a few of these assemblies, he possibly would have produced *two* volumes for perpetuity: Parliamentary Law, Male; and Parliamentary Law, Female.

For example, this could happen *only* at a woman's meeting: The chairman had called the meeting to order. Then her eye fell on a member seated alone in the front row. Handing down a pad and pencil she whispered, "Our secretary is absent today. Will you please keep the minutes of the meeting and give them to me before you leave?" The little woman assented with a nod and a smile. When the meeting ended, she serenely returned the pad and pencil to the chairman and without a word quietly departed. It was later that the chairman read the pinch-hitting secretary's full report: "Minutes of the meeting: Forty minutes and thirty-five seconds."

Are Women Funnier Than Anybody?

Women may not be funnier than men when they preside at a meeting, or write a letter, or give a report or talk on the phone. Let's say again that they are *different*.

For example, what man would have made this report?

The occasion was a large district church convention, and hundreds of women had been mustered for an all-out telephone campaign so that each member in every church received a personal invitation to assemble. When the "doings" were over, the general chairman of the telephone committee arose at the final report meeting and proudly made this announcement:

"I would like to take this opportunity to thank all of you girls from the various churches who were so helpful in our attendance drive. We contacted by phone almost every member in three counties, and had a wonderful response.

"I want especially to congratulate Circle Six from our local church, for I am delighted to report that they furnished more *call girls* for the convention than any other circle! Congratulations Circle Six. Let's have a nice round of applause for these ladies."

Women's announcements are worth examining. These were special jewels shining in a dull world:

Last minute instructions to the Creative Writing Class of the University Women: "I'm not going to mince words with you ladies about the importance of this assignment. Just remember to watch your p's and q's, and for heaven's sake, avoid those clichés like the plague!"

―――――――

Flower show note: "The Men's Garden Club requested that in the Horticulture Division we tag their entries as 'Nemophila maculata' instead of the familiar name of 'Baby Blue-Eyes,' and 'Impatiens Balsamina' instead of 'Touch-me-nots.'"

―――――――

An announcement of note: "To Club members who have joined the 'Slim Down' group: the member who loses the most pounds and inches during the next six weeks will be given an award at the annual banquet, called the 'No Belly Prize.'"

―――――――

Then there was the Investment Club. A polite young man from a brokerage firm had spent a good part of an evening explaining to the ladies the inner workings of the Stock Market. When he completed his well planned talk, he made the error of asking, "Are there any questions?".

There was only one. "I think I speak for our entire group," a member said, "We don't care too much about things like those bears and bulls all going up and down. What we want to know is how much do you think each of us could make if we put in

$10 a week out of our weekly household money in the stock market for the next year?"

———————

And this letter . . . could mere man compose such an explanation?

Dear Mrs. Ware:

Last spring when you spoke at the National Convention I talked with you about coming to our garden club in October. In the meantime, my husband was cleaning out the gutters around our roof. We have lots of pine trees and the gutters were full of pine straw and were sagging. The ladder slipped and he caught on to a section of the gutter that was rotten, and that was how his accident happened. His leg is still in a cast and we have had to enclose the downstairs sun-porch to make a bedroom because he cannot climb the stairs.

This work has taken much longer than we expected and the workmen are still here. Fortunately, there is a bathroom downstairs and we did not have to go to the trouble and expense to add one. If you have ever had any major repairs made to an old house then you understand what I am talking about.

However, I would like to explain this to you. The bathroom is on the back of the house and quite a distance from the sunporch. In other words, my husband has to come through the living room, down the hall, and past the kitchen to get to the bath. He is now using a wheel chair and crutches and you can see that this is sometimes inconvenient.

We have 40 members in our garden club to which you were asked to speak in October. My husband (who still doesn't feel too good) is of the opinion that this is a large crowd to entertain here considering the work going on and the location of the bathroom.

I hope this will NOT inconvenience you and maybe you could come and talk to us in the spring. Just this morning I talked with the man at the lumber yard and he informs me that the window frames have not even been shipped; so, I do hope you will understand my position. Most sincerely, E. W. B.

———

There are also lop-sided feminine telephone conversations that could be recorded for posterity. This time there happened to be a pencil handy. These notes were taken during a busy dinner hour . . . that crucial 6 to 7 p.m. pandemonium period when housewives find themselves in the usual end-of-the-day frenzy. It went like this:

SHE: Hello. Are you the Mrs. Ware who teaches parliamentary law?

ME: Yes, that's right.

SHE: Well, I'm in a spot and need some help. Can you tell me what to do?

ME: I don't know, but I can try. Who is this, by the way?

SHE: Oh, you don't know me, but I saw you on the TV talking about parliamentary law, and I thought you might help me.

ME: What's your problem?

SHE: Well, it's this way. You see, I really didn't want the job, you understand that, don't you?

ME: What job?

SHE: Oh, I'm first vice-president for the Meadow Hill PTA. I guess you read about in the paper.

ME: Well, no, I don't believe I did. But, if you already have the job, I don't see how I can help you?

"IS THERE ANYTHING IN OUR CONSTITUTION ABOUT MOVING EVERYTHING DOWN TO THE SECOND VICE PRESIDENT IF YOU LEAVE TOWN ?"

SHE: Well, it's sort of a funny situation, but I'll see if I can explain it to you. I've got to decide tonight.

ME: Will you excuse me a minute while I turn off my dinner on the stove. Things are starting to boil over.

SHE: Sure, but I won't be a minute . . . but I do need your advice.

ME: If you'll explain what it is I can help you with I'd be glad to try to . . .

SHE: I can't exactly explain it, but it has to do with what this woman said I was supposed to do.

ME: What woman?

SHE: Oh, our president. She's moving out of town next week, you know.

ME: No, I didn't know that.

SHE: Army. They never give these people enough notice. My husband was in the Navy, and they're not much better. When we were transferred from California, they didn't give us but two days notice, and I had already arranged to have my little boy's tonsils out that next week.

ME: Er . . . would it be asking too much for you to tell me just what it is that I can assist you with? I'm in rather a spot here in the kitchen and the timer is buzzing on the oven. Would you rather I call you back?

SHE: It won't take a minute. It was just that this woman—she's sort of bossy, you know, and she seems to think the first vice-president automatically takes over the president's duties, and I can't do that. I've got four kids, and I'm already program chairman. Now, exactly what does the rule book say when the first vice-president is also the program chairman? Is there anything about the second vice-president taking over the other person's job if that person already has another job?

ME: What does it say about it in your club by-laws?

SHE: Now, that's the whole thing. We can't find the book.

ME: You mean the Robert's Rules of Order book?

SHE: Heavens no, we didn't even try to figure that thing out. No, I mean our club book that has the by-laws in it.

ME: Each group makes its own set of by-laws about things like that, and you would have to find that before you can make any decision.

SHE: That's what I want you to do; make the decision.

ME: But it's not up to me or anyone else to make the decision. You'll either have to find the book with the by-laws or bring it up and vote on it at your next meeting.

SHE: Oh, for goodness sake. We wouldn't dream of going to all that bother. I'll just tell them that Robert's Rules says to move everything down to the second vice-president. That makes sense, doesn't it?

ME: No, I'm afraid not. At least, well, I've never heard of any such a rule as that.

SHE: Wonderful, I can't tell you how much I appreciate all you've done. My calling you right here at dinner time and all that . . . but this has certainly solved all my problems . . . thanks a million . . . 'bye now.

. . . And goodbye to you, my dear. . . whoever you are.

APPENDIX

Instant Parliamentary Law
or
Parliamentary Rules Made Easy

In this little Appendix we have compiled the correct **How To** rules apart from the **How Not To's.** Completely (well, almost completely) sequestered from anything that smacks of fun and frolic, we give you this important and necessary sector . . . **What you should know about parliamentary law,** right in your own Appendix.

You may have it extracted, or you may prefer to staple or tape it together. Better still, commit it to memory. If you belong to **anything,** or if you ever hope to join any club or organization, may we suggest that you cherish this little segment. Refer to it often and accurately, so that you will never be guilty of some things that are recorded in the preceding pages. So, dear ladies, you will know what to do . . .

> When members attend in a quorum
> Be sure, Madame Chairman, don't bore 'em.
> When Club woes they unravel,
> Just pound with your gavel
> And floor 'em with forum decorum.

Parliamentary Procedure for Informal Groups

Heaven's first law is ORDER, and the same rule applies to parliamentary procedure. Often unskilled officers, as well as some members, feel that this is some wordy witches' brew, concocted to promote confusion in an organization. In truth, it is the other way around. The only way to avoid such a jumble is for each member to have some comprehension of the mechanics of parliamentary rules, so that business sessions are expedited rather than obstructed.

Correct procedure in the conducting of meetings is as important as rules of grammar in speaking or writing. Regardless of what the amateur parliamentarian might consider inanity, some knowledge of the science of parliamentary law and the principles upon which it is based, will often solve quickly and satisfactorily many problems which are likely to arise at a meeting. Such principles as courtesy and justice to all, handling one thing at a time, the rule of the majority and the rights of the minority, are indispensable for smooth sailing, even in a more informal group. It is concerning these informal organizations, in which the majority of women are involved, that only the simplest of rules are needed.

Glossary: Let's Learn the Terms

The Constitution. The first thing any organization requires is a set of rules, i.e., a constitution and by-laws. This should be simple in form and contain only such provisions as are expected to be permanent. The constitution should contain the name, time of meeting, object of the society, qualifications and number of members, names and duties of officers and the way and time they are to be elected, and all committees.

In the by-laws there should be set forth the number or percentage of members to decide a quorum; the rights and duties of officers and members; dues and assessments; the order of business (the agenda); the parliamentary authority to be used;

and how amendments are to be made. The more concise this is made, the better it will be understood.

The Chairman. The person responsible for conducting the meeting in an orderly fashion, and as speedily as possible, is the chairman or president, or whatever the presiding officer may be called. (One organization, for example, is headed up by the Loyal Worthy Grand Queen Mother, and such a title definitely deserves deference.) The chairman may not make, second, or debate a motion while she is occupying the "chair," or the seat of authority. One parliamentary guide refers to the chairman as the "head referee," which she is.

Motions. All business is introduced in a meeting by means of a "motion," which is an idea, a plan or suggestion. Someone must second that motion before there can be any debate or discussion on it. A member should rise, address the chair (presiding officer), and by voice or a nod be recognized before she speaks. By that she "obtains the floor," or the opportunity to speak uninterrupted. To save time and to avoid misunderstanding, it is a good idea to write out a long and detailed motion, and hand it to the chairman.

One of the most common causes of chaos in women's meetings is when the members do not understand this ruling, or forget that there is a motion on the floor which has not been acted upon, and go off into tangents of discussions. These are things that chairmen must guard against carefully, for a band of enthusiastic women can give birth to more ideas in an unguarded moment than a prolific guppy can reproduce little guppies in an aquarium.

There are four different kinds of motions: main, subsidiary, privileged, and incidental. When the average woman who has joined something reads this, she is apt to toss in the sponge. But, if she will take a deep breath and plunge head first into a few more sentences, she will discover that this is not as complicated as it sounds. For example:

(1) **Main Motions.** These are motions which introduce a subject to the assembly, and are made only when no

other question is pending. (For example, someone may have moved that the club piano be painted pink, and the motion is seconded. Then before the vote is cast, there might be an amendment to the motion that the piano stool be painted blue.) Amendments are made by inserting or by striking out words or phrases of the original motion, or striking out and inserting by substitution.

(2) **Subsidiary Motions.** These are motions to amend (or change) motions. This happens when the members wish to dispose of a motion in some way other than voting it down or passing on it at that meeting. This can be done by (a) "laying it on the table," (when it is undebatable, unamendable, and requires a majority vote); (b) limiting the debate or referring it to a committee; or (c) postponing it indefinitely. When a question goes past these elementary rules, then it is necessary for the parliamentarian to refer to **Robert's Rules of Order Revised,** or some similar rule book.* It is a rare case when problems like this arise in a small and informal group.

(3) **Privileged Motions.** These are motions of importance because they are allowed to interrupt consideration of other questions at hand. These usually include such things as time to adjourn or recess for lunch, or a question of privilege to interrupt. For example, during a discussion a member might arise, be recognized by the chair, and inform the chairman that the loud-speaker system had switched off, or that the furnace was about to blow up (an actual case). These are privileged motions and are not debatable.

(4) **Incidental Motions.** These are problems that arise and must be decided before the business is presented. These motions have no definite rank and are considered incidental. For example, a member may say,

* Recommended: "An Elementary Course in Parliamentary Procedure," by Herberta A. Leonardy, 239 Fluvia Ave., Coral Gables, Fla. 33134.

"Madame Chairman, I rise to a point of order," when a noisy member begins passing out the year books during the business session, which could be very disconcerting to the chairman or to members attempting to listen and to keep order.

A Quorum. This is usually the majority of members who must be present to vote on a motion to have it pass. Most clubs list a specific number or percentage of members in their by-laws who must be present or must send in an absentee ballot.

Resolutions. These are expressions of the club's policy or their attitude or action or intention on a certain question. Such a resolution must be moved and seconded and voted upon. (For example, a garden club might want to go on public record that they do not want all of the century-old oak trees surrounding the courthouse cut down by the City Beautification Committee.)

Voting. If a ballot is to be cast regarding election of officers, new members, or motions on any business, it is advisable for the chairman to announce whether the voting will be done by those in favor saying "aye," those opposed "no"; by secret ballot; by a show of hands; or by a standing vote.

On a tie vote the motion is lost. If there is a majority of one, the chair may vote, thus making it a tie, and then declare the motion lost. In written ballot the voting may continue in the event of a tie vote until there is a majority.

Let's Begin the Meeting

The Agenda. The order of business, or the agenda, is the first and most important part of any meeting. This is a guide for the presiding officer to go by, and the wise chairman plans ahead what business is to take place, and estimates the approximate time each item will consume. Everyone is anxious to complete the business sessions as quickly as possible and to move on to more interesting matters. (In women's groups, often the very members who are most impatient to scurry through the reports will linger at the tea table until the candles dissolve into forlorn lumps of tallow. These members somehow regard the business sessions as necessary evils, which they can be, if they are disorganized and take up an unreasonable amount of time.)

A simple idea to follow is:

(1) Call meeting to order
(2) Devotional and Pledge of Allegiance to the Flag (if customary)
(3) Roll call, and minutes (Secretary)
(4) Correspondence (Corresponding Secretary)
(5) Treasurer's report
(6) Reports of standing (permanent) committees
(7) Reports of special committees
(8) Unfinished or old business
(9) New business
(10) Motion to adjourn

For further study, see **Robert's Rules of Order, Revised—** page 262.

The Call to Order. The chairman opens the meeting by saying "Will the meeting please come to order." If there is no gavel available to rap for attention, she should improvise with an ashtray, spoon or glass, so as to let the members know in a business-like way that conversation must cease. This calling to order should be done at the appointed time, regardless of the number of members present. This establishes a precedent of beginning and ending on time, and will generally assure a prompt attendance at further meetings. If it is customary for a meeting to begin late, the members are less apt to be on time, a habit which gets progressively worse as the year goes on.

Recording Secretary. Usually the chairman calls first upon the secretary to call the roll and read the minutes or the account of the last meeting. Next, she will ask, "Are there any additions or corrections to these minutes?" If there are none, she will continue, "If not, the minutes stand approved as read." Some clubs prefer to dispense with the roll call and the reading of the minutes and have mimeographed copies of the minutes passed out, or to have the secretary announce only the most important events. (For example, not too many people are interested to recall that at the last meeting the members stood and sang

Hymn No. 323, "Oh Beautiful Day," but they like to be reminded that they voted to plant a twenty-foot magnolia tree in the church garden.)

The secretary should always have her book of minutes, by-laws, and some parliamentary guide at hand, in case a question does arise. Many valuable records are often not inserted in club books because notes are carelessly scribbled on backs of envelopes and never recorded. The minutes are not concluded any more with "Respectfully submitted" before the secretary's signature. (That is now passé.)

Corresponding Secretary. This office may be combined with that of the recording secretary if the organization does not have much correspondence. This officer's report can easily be condensed and only the highlights of the communications mentioned. (For example, instead of reading a two-page typewritten letter from the Humane Society, the secretary can announce that the group has been invited to attend the Pet Show Tuesday at seven o'clock, and list the kinds of pets to be entered.) With possibly a dozen or more letters and requests at hand, this brief condensation brings into focus the most significant facts, and catches the member's attention more successfully by its brevity.

Treasurer. The treasurer collects the dues and keeps an accurate account of collections and expenditures, and gives an up-to-date report of this at each meeting. In larger groups she should have a finance and budget committee to work with her, with books being set up along the lines of bookkeeping practices. She should give receipts for all money paid in, and keep copies of all bills and accounts paid out. In the interest of time, some treasurers only report the balance on hand and do not go into detail on every penny spent, but these records are open for inspection by any officers or members interested. Some groups hand out a mimeographed treasurer's report, as most women are vague when it comes to keeping figures in their heads.

Committees. Standing committees are those that are permanently connected with the organization, like Ways and Means, Finance, By-laws, Club House, etc. Special committees are those appointed for some special event and only function that one time, e.g., Christmas Party Committee, or some fund raising project that takes place once a year.

Unfinished Business. Business carried over from a previous meeting.

New Business. New ideas or plans to be placed before the group either for discussion or to be put in the form of a motion.

Adjourn. A motion is usually made when the business is completed or postponed, and the meeting is dismissed, and like this book, it STANDS ADJOURNED.

A fourth generation native of Atlanta, Georgia, Runa Erwin Ware was educated at Washington Seminary and at Hollins College, Virginia. She and her husband, Fred, have moved and traveled extensively. Seven years were spent in Australia with General Motors before settling in Augusta.

Active in church, civic and club affairs, and in teaching parliamentary law, Mrs. Ware was often amused at the wacky things women say and do at meetings, and began jotting down in shorthand much of this "candid chatter." Some of these gems were used to sparkle up a speech she gave at a convention of the National Council of Garden Clubs Inc. The response was so overwhelming that within the year she was invited to speak to over a hundred organizations, including many men's groups, e.g., Rotary, Kiwanis, Lions, etc. This book is the answer to numerous requests for more peeking behind the scenes at women's clubs.

Mrs. Ware first began writing on the *Atlanta Constitution,* and later was Book Review editor of the *Augusta Chronicle.* The Wares have two sons—one an engineer with Lockheed, and the other a Presbyterian minister and amateur golfer—and five grandchildren.

She is currently working on another book in this same light vein . . . making merry with life on a cruise ship, where things are not always as enchanting as the travel brochures proclaim.

ABOUT THE ARTIST

Charles Wickersham III or "Wick", the talented young man who drew the clever cartoons, was a native of Washington, Ga., and a 1960 graduate of the University of Georgia. His untimely death in a car accident at the age of 28 has cut short the life of a brilliant and dedicated young man who had a delightful sense of humor, great potential, and who possibly would have been one of the top artists to emerge from the University's outstanding and nationally known School of Art.